Copyright © 2014 by Yetta Yvette

Third Edition published June 2021
by Indies United Publishing House, LLC

Cover Art by iPanda

All rights reserved. Without limiting the rights under copyright reserved above; no part of this publication may be reproduced stored in or introduced into a retrieval system or transmitted in any form or by any means (electronic, mechanical, photocopying, recording or otherwise) without the prior written permission of both the copyright owner and the above publisher of this book.

Paperback ISBN: 978-1-64456-315-1
Mobi ISBN: 978-1-64456-316-8
ePub ISBN: 978-1-64456-317-5

Library of Congress Control Number: 2021938533

INDIES UNITED PUBLISHING HOUSE, LLC
P.O. BOX 3071
QUINCY, IL 62305-3071
www.indiesunited.net

Dedication

A special, very special dedication goes to my sixth-grade Catskill Elementary School teacher, Mrs. Barbara Watters (R.I.P.), who gave me encouragement with her words, "Baby, you can do whatever you put your heart and mind to." I love you for that, and I appreciate it gratefully.

Recognition

I take great pleasure in writing the story of my life on the pages of this book. It's like therapy to my soul and a chapter of my life. That is and will always be so memorable. I have to admit, it has shaped me into becoming a strong, black woman and entrepreneur. Many people wondered why, and they would ask, "Why are you so driven?" Now you can understand why. Thanks for reading my story! This book is dedicated to those who lost their other half and feel that they can't go on. Just know that with each passing day, it gets better. Like what they say, time heals all wounds. A special thanks to all my English teachers, especially, Mrs. McMurray. The Pratt family, my beautiful mother, handsome father, my lovely sisters, all the people who are a part of my life story, and God, who strengthened me when I was weak.

Table of Contents

Prelude
- *Love Is Love*..v
- *Life*...vi
- *Inspirational Quotes*..vii

The Diary of Yetta Yvette...1
Introduction...6
Day One...9
Our First Dinner Date..19
The Attraction..29
The Rendezvous: Part 1..31
The Secret Is Out..38
The Rendezvous: Part 2..41
The Meet with the Parents...43
Someone Has to Lose...46
The Transformation...48
My 27th Birthday...50
Trouble with My Best Friends......................................52
My Storm..55
My Proposal..61
Here Comes Another Storm...64
Mister's Birthday..73
The Promise..76
Without a Sound..81
Our Last Intimate Moment..84
The Funeral..86
Who is Mister?..89
Life After Mister...91
My Guardian Angel..106
Life's Uncertainties..108
Learning How to Love Again.....................................113
Intimacy...125
- *My Words of Inspiration*......................................*131*
- *The Advice*..*132*

In Loving Memory
"Mister"
R.I.P.
My Mentor
The Rose in a Concrete World

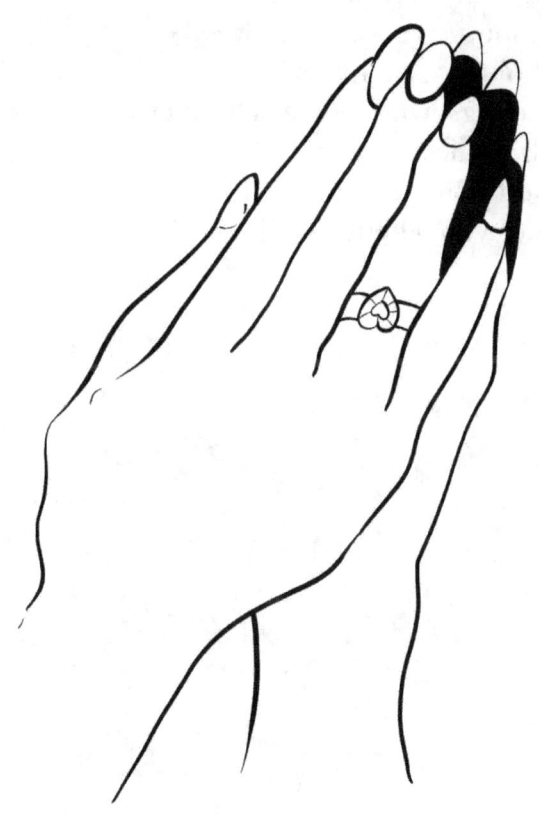

Love Is Love

A Poem
by Yetta Yvette

Love has no boundaries,
love is unconditional,
love doesn't discriminate or eliminate,
when you truly love someone.
It's not about Age, Race, or Creed;
love is about two people with
strong feelings, who need each other to survive.
Love tells no lies;
when you know it's true,
love makes you a better you!

Life

There will be stops and road blocks...Pot holes (negative people) to avoid, but you have to not let it detour you toward a direction of giving up. Strive and continue to progress down the journey of life. Before you know it, you will have arrived to your destination.

Inspirational Quotes

Don't judge a day by the happiness, you take from it. Judge it by the happiness you bring into it. It is not because things are difficult that we o not dare, it is because we do not dare that things are difficult.
—Seneca

What the mind can conceive, it can achieve. —Napoleon Hill

All dreams can come true-if we have the courage to pursue them. —Walt Disney

It is never too late to be what you might have been. —George Elliott

The best years of life are the ones in which you decide your problems are your own. You do not blame them on your mother, the ecology, or the president. You realize that you control your own destiny.
—Albert Ellis

There are only two ways to live your life. One is as though nothing is a miracle. The other is as though everything is a miracle. —Albert Einstein

Great minds discuss ideas. Average minds discuss events. Small minds discuss people. —Eleanor Roosevelt

If opportunity doesn't knock, build a door. —Milton Berle

When you can't change the direction of the wind- adjust your sails. —H Jackson Brown Jr.

Your time is limited, don't waste it living someone's life. Don't be trapped by dogma, which is living the results of other's people thinking. Don't let the noise of other's opinion drowned your own inner voice. And most important, have the courage to follow your heart and intuition, they somehow already know what you truly want to become. Everything else is secondary. —Steve Jobs

Gravitation is not responsible for people falling in love. —Albert Einstein

Never let opportunities pass you by. Be thankful for what you have; you'll end up having more. If you concentrate on what you don't have, you will, never, never have enough. —Oprah Winfrey

Those who wish to sing, always find a song. Courage is not the absence of fear, but rather the judgment that something else is more important than fear. —James Hollingworth

Luck is what happens when preparation meets opportunity. —Seneca

A life is not important except in the impact it has on other lives. —Jackie Robinson

Watch your thoughts they become words. Watch your words they become actions. Watch your actions; they become habit. Watch your habits; they become character. Watch your character; it becomes your destiny. —Lao Tzu

Life is tough, but it's tougher when you're stupid. —John Wayne

The hardest thing to see is what is in front of your eyes.

Age Ain't Nothing but a Number

YETTA YVETTE

INDIES UNITED PUBLISHING HOUSE, LLC

The Diary of Yetta Yvette

At birth, I was given the name Yetta Yvette. For those who think that they may know me, actually you haven't the slightest clue. This is the life and the diary Of Yetta Yvette. According to the Old English meaning, Yetta means "to give." Generous. A name that I eventually will live up to in my life. I was born a Leo baby in the month of August. At eight months old, my family left the dirty south of Shreveport, Louisiana, and migrated to Los Angeles, California. From this point on in my life, I grew up to be a West Coast California girl, my mother and father's first creation, and the eldest of my two younger sisters. I was my mother's little helper, as she would call it, and my daddy's little girl.

At the early age of five, I was struck by tragedy. I was viciously mauled by my older cousin, German Sheppard. They called him "Champ." The screams and cries of my mother terrified me more than the terrible incident. I was rushed to a nearby hospital. Doctors worked relentlessly on my badly scarred, bruised, and swollen face. During my recovery, I had to wear bandages, and it was very difficult for me to eat food. God was looking out over me though, because just a centimeter more from the dog bite, and I would have been blind in one eye. I cringe at the thought. I have stitch marks as a reminder of that day. I was so blessed for a second chance. Even after that catastrophe, I am proud to say that I am still an animal lover. In fact, I received my dog Pepper as a gift from a very special person, when it was just five months old. Now, he is going on fifteen years old. My other dog—Stumpy Thump Thump, that's what I call him—I got him from a co-worker when he was just a puppy. He is going on nine years old now. I raised both of them, from puppies to grown dogs. I love my two dogs to death.

After six to eight months of healing from the incident, I was already changing my sisters' diapers, making baby bottles, and just doing whatever was necessary to assist my mother. I would soon have the responsibilities of being a role model to my two younger sisters. Because of that role, I learned leadership. As a young girl, I always aspired to be in the spotlight. My mother always kept my sisters and me participating in dancing, sports, Girl Scouts, and other various activities, to keep our young minds active.

Church was also a part of our world. When Sunday morning came along, the white church bus would pick us up at exactly eight o'clock in the morning. We were taught the word of God; our faith was Baptist, and I was even baptized. That was also the time when I experienced my very first crush on a boy. He was two years older than me, and was such a cutie. It was always fun attending church, especially knowing that he was going to be there. His presence always gave me butterflies inside. I was so nervous around him that every time the bus pulled up to his house, I always prayed, "Oh please, I hope he will be going." There were also a few times when he didn't show up. I was so disappointed.

My mother never had any problems with me when it came to going to church, and she eventually found out the real reason. She didn't have to force me to say it, like some parents would do.

At age thirteen, I went to modeling school. I anticipated a career in show business. My ultimate dream at the time was to become a huge supermodel, who would work the runways with the latest fashion, but I fell short. I only grew to be five feet and four inches tall. My height wouldn't allow it, and it crushed my heart to pieces. I then began developing a strong love for the game of basketball. I played in some neighborhood parks, and I loved it.

Once I enrolled in junior high school, I became a huge fan of drill team and was accepted to Black Heritage Club. I sang in the school choir and learned to play the guitar. In 1987, I attended Hollywood High School, a performing arts school that mostly focuses on the developments of a career in show business. I was still aspiring to shine like a "star." Acting, dancing, and singing were my main priorities. I remember waiting at the bus stop at five forty-five in the morning for my bus to come and pick me up for school. The school was an hour and a half away from my house. I did my eight hours of school and would be back on that bus. On my way home, I had to do my homework on the bus because by the time I made it home it was already seven thirty in the evening. And before you know it, it was time to do it all over again.

The experience was like the television show Fame. Fame. It was what I desired, what I dreamed of. But then my grades started to take a turn for the worst. My parents took notice of it, and the next thing I knew, I was withdrawn from that school and was now attending a nearby school. I hated the switch, but I had to adjust myself to the changes. Eventually, my grades made it back up to As, Bs, and Cs, and I became very active at my new school.

Once again, I was able to sing in the school choir, have lots of fun in the drill team, and attend the Friday night football games. Once when graduation was near, I remember I had a teacher who asked me, "What would you like to do more than anything in the world once you graduate from high school?"

At that very moment, I knew my career path. I decided I wanted to make big bucks, lots of money. I wanted to be a businesswoman. At that time, I knew that I wanted to be extremely successful with a purpose in my life.

Upon graduating from high school, my mother and father gave me a trip to Hawaii. That adventure with Stacey made me really realize the kind of lifestyle that I had to have. We encountered fun times together, and after I graduated from high school, I enrolled at a two-year junior college. I started working part-time for a real estate company, a retail store, and a fast-food chain. I was doing it all at once, and sometimes I was working two jobs at a time and then off to school at night. I would be so exhausted, but I had to keep myself awake, so I could absorb the lesson.

At age twenty-two, I finally figured it all out. The line of business I wanted to go into was cosmetology. I was fascinated by cosmetology because when you look good, it makes you feel better about yourself; you'll have a positive attitude and outlook in life. I took facial makeup courses at Universal Studios and enrolled in a Cosmetology course. The course was for two years. I wanted to be an entrepreneur and have my own business. Once I finished the course, I took the exam, and after two tries, I was a licensed cosmetologist. I was doing hair and having fun with my styles. I did this for a while, and then a position opened up that allowed me to make more money. At that time, I was twenty-four years old, and I had a tattoo of my nickname, Lady Y, with two-dollar signs on my shoulder, valuing myself in the highest manner like money.

My dreams have never been to live an average lifestyle. I always desired to live over the top. I craved for it. Like a celebrity, I knew what I wanted, and I was on my way to it. I had the fire in my eyes, and I was hungry for it… Success!

Introduction

I was a student at a two-year junior college and working at a drugstore part-time. I was trying to find my place in this crazy world, and it all started with a pink referral card that my younger sister had referred me onto; she worked at the employment office. I had been on so many job interviews, and every time I was always so damn disappointed and frustrated with the outcome. On this one particular day, my mother found out the news from my sister and somehow convinced me to check into it.

The position was for a full-time dispatch clerk typist for a trucking company. The position started out at eight dollars an hour, and the job duties included answering the telephones, dispatching, and a little bookkeeping. My mother was very persistent with her nagging, and she would say, "C'mon! It wouldn't hurt for you to find out about it." So that afternoon, I called to schedule an interview, and again I felt like I was only wasting my time. The following day, I was on my way to the interview. I tried to think positive, but in my heart, I was feeling discouraged before I could even get into the front door. I met up with the interviewer. She was a woman. I filled out the job application, and once I finished it, she interviewed me.

The first question she asked me was, "Do you

have any trucking experience?"

My response was no, and she gave me a funny look. At this point, I started to feel pretty inadequate.

She stressed to me that she needed someone with trucking experience. Once the interview concluded, I thanked her for taking the time out to even consider me for the position. Part of me felt terrible about the interview, and the other part felt good because the business was being operated and ran by people like me—black. I walked out of the building, and I could feel someone staring at me. That was when I saw a man sitting at the dispatch desk. He was dispatching truckers to their destination and waiting for truckers coming in with their truck loads. I was so proud to have seen this, and I walked out of the building feeling more motivated and confident. I smiled and said hello. He also smiled and said hello.

This is the beginning of my story.

Some weeks passed by, and I was preparing and studying for a business exam. I was thirsting for success very badly, but I had no idea how I was going to achieve it. I was only working part-time, and I needed a full-time job to help me pursue my education. I didn't hear anything from the trucking company interview for a while, but on that day, I received a call. My prayers were finally answered. I was informed to come in for a second interview.

Back then when you were instructed to come back for a second interview, nine times out of ten it meant that you got the job. But how could it be? I didn't have any trucking experience.

It was a Wednesday, and I was on my way to my second interview. I entered the building with my nerves racing. My adrenaline was flowing so strongly, and I was overwhelmed with anxiety. I met up with the interviewer again, and she asked me a few follow-up questions. I was offered the position.

Wow! I couldn't believe it. I was told that I had no experience and that trucking experience is what was mandatory. What's with the sudden change? I didn't know, so I took it for what it was worth and accepted my blessing. I was so excited I couldn't wait to get home so I could tell my mother the news and make her proud of me. She knew that I was on the verge of giving up.

I walked in the house and told her the good news, and she congratulated me, saying, "You were thinking of not going. See, just when you think you know everything…but only God knows your fate."

Day One

I was extremely nervous; I arrived about fifteen minutes earlier than my scheduled eight o'clock-shift. I met with the staff and was shown all around the office. I met this cool chick name Gloria. A Hispanic dispatch receptionist who made me feel really comfortable. I trained and trained and learned the ins and outs of the operation. It was very difficult to catch on in the beginning. There was so much information to learn. I thought to myself, how was I going to be able to remember all of it, plus school? Everyone was so friendly and helpful though, and most of all, patient.

A couple of months in and I was receiving constant stares again. The stares were coming from that man, who happened to be the owner. He was a middle-aged man with salt and pepper hair. He had eyes that could intimidate and the demeanor of strength. It was like watching Victor Newman from the soap opera The Young and the Restless. He wasn't for any bullshit; he was tough. But on certain days, he would treat his entire staff to orange juice, including his wife, who was the interviewer. I guessed he wanted to make sure our immune systems were up. He didn't want us to catch a cold, get sick, and have to be off from work. For me, apple juice was always my favorite, and he was very gentleman-like about it. He always opened it and put a straw in it for me. At first, I didn't think anything of it. I just thought he was being friendly and nice, but I constantly kept receiving more and more special treatment from him, and I started to feel self-conscious about it.

The next day, he walked in the office very aggressively. It was ten o'clock in the morning, and his wife Sharon, Gloria, and I were completing some direct billing documents. He walked up to my desk, with a smile on his face, and said, "Yvette, can I borrow you for a few minutes?" Putting his finger on his head, he added, "Oh yeah, please bring your legal pad and a black pen."

"Hi! Yes, sure!" I replied.

He directed me over to his office for some dictation. He pulled back my seat, and I sat down in a chair in front of his desk. I politely thanked him, and after doing so, he pulled back his chair from behind his desk. He sat and began the conversation.

"Okay, Yvette, I need to send this company a business letter," he said. "There is a discrepancy with billing, and I need this to be rectified. Do you think you can do that for me?"

"Of course, I can do it!" I responded.

"Okay, let's get started."

During the dictation, his lingering eyes were traveling up and down my body. It wasn't the kind of stares that a boss gives his secretary. This was totally different. His eyes were undressing me, piece by piece, as if my white blouse and black skirt were slowly coming off. While this was going on, I was occasionally repeating the dictation, and once it was completed, I walked over back to my office. I began typing the business documents for him.

I knew his behavior was very inappropriate, but I never wanted to report him for sexual harassment, because if I were to do that, it meant that I would be pulling us down. His business was predominantly operated by Blacks and Hispanics. I just couldn't do it. I'm strongly all about Black empowerment, so I chose to ignore it. I was strictly about that business, and that was the way I was intending to keep it—professional.

It was around lunchtime some weeks later when he told Sharon that he wanted to eat his favorite from McDonald's, which was a Fish Fillet or a "Fish Burger," as he would call it. Although his wife had packed a lunch for him, he didn't want to eat it. On that day, it was becoming crystal clear to me. Asking his wife to buy him a meal from McDonald's would only be his way of getting her out of the office so he could make his move.

She left the building and drove off speedily in her black jeep, and it was only him and me. Everyone else in the office had stepped out for lunch. Within a minute of her leaving, I received a buzz on my phone, and his deep like Barry White voice started speaking into the intercom. "Hi, Yvette! How are you today?" he asked.

"I'm doing well, thank you." I replied.

"I need to speak to you." My heart started pounding. I saw him approaching my office, and I wanted to give him the benefit of the doubt. What's going on here? Did I screw up on an invoice? Am I in some kind of trouble? By the tone of his voice, it sounded very serious. I was terrified of this man.

But when he entered my office he started a conversation with me. He asked me questions about school, my major, and my goals in life. Did I have a boyfriend? Yes, he asked me that and, of course, I was reluctant to tell him about that. At the time, I didn't really have a serious relationship. The guy whom I considered to be a boyfriend at the time was just a knucklehead.

My heart was yearning to be in love with a man, and my boyfriend just couldn't understand me—what I wanted in a man and my emotional needs as a woman. We weren't compatible at all. "Yes, I do," I still told him anyway. He went on to tell me that he could assist me with my career and help me advance to the top of the corporate ladder.

In most cases, it is not what you know, but who you know. I did hear that quote many times, before, and I thought, ugh! I know where this could be heading. I was cool, sharp, and I always played nonchalant about it. I was trying my best to keep this married man in his place. Was he happy in his marriage? I didn't know, but I soon found out.

My dress code was very simple. I wore long dresses that reached below the knee, and even with leggings sometimes. I never wore clothes that showed too much because being too revealing or provocative was never my style. My mother and father raised my sisters and me that way. We were raised to be classy, young ladies. I always tried to be respectful to Sharon.

Monday through Friday, there were more and more signs of his affection for me. I had a lot of stress at school, with English papers due, and the financial woes of trying to pay my bills. It felt like a ton of bricks weighing on my shoulders. My mother used to always tell me, "You should stay a kid as long as you can, because being a grown-up is not easy." When I was a kid, I couldn't understand it but as a young adult, I understood every bit of what she meant. I was super-stressed.

On that day, Mister pushed my buttons to the extreme, and I had all that I could tolerate from him.

~

It was around four thirty in the afternoon, and I was pretty exhausted from a long day at work. I was winding down going into relaxation mode. I was so ready to get off from work and go home when he walked into my office. I was organizing some files on my messy desk, and he was standing in the doorway of my office.

"So, Yvette, how was your day?" he asked me.

"It went well, thank you," I replied. I always kept our conversations brief and to the point. He went on to ask me a few more questions, about all the information that I was learning within the company, for instance, what dock terminal is Hanjin?

See, all the container terminals had numbers

that represented them. I knew some of them, but it was so difficult trying to remember all of them, and my brain was on overload because of school. So, it slipped my memory, and I answered it incorrectly. He looked at me, and by the look on his face, you would have thought that I was on trial or something. I was being drilled, and he was my drill sergeant, and at the same time, I was feeling so intimidated and humiliated. I was shrinking in my seat. I was feeling smaller and smaller and probably because I was being quizzed in front of the entire staff.

No one could help me out with any answers. It was like I was in school and wearing a dunce hat. I felt so stupid. What in the hell was wrong with him? How could he embarrass me like this? From that point on, it made me reconsider my position with the company. Every day there was always some shit going on.

With all of his flirtation, Sharon noticed it too, but instead of taking it out on him, setting him straight, and putting him in his place, she always checked me instead. She had more of an attitude toward me. She would harass me for everything. When I made an error with work, she would really emphasize it. Clearly, I wasn't happy working there anymore. I had about enough of it.

On my drive home, I contemplated hard. I was at a crossroads. Should I go to the right, meaning quit and look for another job? Or should I go to the left and stay there and take it? I already invested about nine months with the company, and I needed this job to help me afford school, but at the same time, it was stressing the hell out of me. What good is having a job with high pressure stress if it's going to keep me from being focused on my long-term career? It didn't make any kind of sense to me because it was only going to reflect on my grades, anyways. I needed to discuss this with someone.

When I made it home, I spilled it all out to my mother. She suggested that I should at least talk to my boss before making a quick decision to quit. So, I listened. Instead of resigning without any explanation, I took my mother's advice. I arranged for a meeting with Sharon so we could clear up the situation.

I was humiliated from the embarrassment. The day came for me to get it off my chest. I was fuming inside. It was the morning and I was waiting for Sharon to come in. She entered the building about 9:30 a.m. I walked up to her and I told her, "I need to speak to you in private." She looked at me with doubt. We walked back to the Mister's office. She slammed the door behind her and we both sat down.

She said, "Okay, Yvette. What's up?"

I told her the whole situation of what occurred the day before; the way I had felt total embarrassment in front of the staff. I said to her, "I can no longer work here. I refuse to be treated in such a way by Mister. So, here's my two-week resignation."

She looked at me in disbelief. Deep down inside, I know there was a part of her that would be delighted for me to leave so I wouldn't be a threat to her anymore. She responded by saying, "Yvette, I am sure he didn't mean it. You know, he carries a lot of stress on him all the time. Maybe you're just interpreting it wrong. I will speak to him about it as soon as he gets in here before you make an irrational decision to leave your position."

I agreed to it.

Mister normally strolls in the office around 10:30 a.m. I looked up at the clock, and out the door to see him walking in the office. Sharon called him over to the other office. They were in there discussing the issue for about fifteen minutes. They both returned to my office. He signaled with his hand to me to come with him to his office for a discussion.

I was nervous but I had to express my feelings. I was hurting inside. I sat down in my chair. He sat in his. He said, "Okay, I hear that you are resigning. First off, let me apologize for yesterday. I didn't mean anything by it. Sorry that you took offense to it. But it was never my intention to shame or belittle you. I have been under so much stress lately. Sometimes I can go overboard redirecting that stress to the wrong person. But by all means, no harm intended. You can't leave me now. I need you here. So now what is your decision? Please stay!"

"Okay, I will accept your apology. It did offend me to the point it brought tears to my eyes because I don't like to feel inferior and it was exactly how I felt."

"My only intention is to make you the best you

can be."

So, I reconsidered, and kept my position. I continued on working there for about three more months until I began to get fed up with Sharon. His flirtation was uncontrollable. He never hid it and was always upfront with it. Many of times, right in front of Sharon. It would cause her to react in such a way. It got to a point that I just couldn't work there any longer. So, my final decision was to leave for good.

But instead of acknowledging the real issue at hand, I informed both of them that school had became too demanding. I needed a part time job instead of working full time. They agreed on my final decision. Sharon baked a pan of carrot cake, and they gave me a farewell party. I appreciated their kindness.

At the same time, I didn't even have another job lined up but I had about five thousand saved up in the bank. I did what I had to do. I just wanted to be comfortable at work again. A month went by, the phone rang. It was Sharon from the trucking company, "How are you?"

"Good thanks," I said hesitantly.

She called because Mister wanted to speak to me. She immediately put him on the line. He invited me to their son's wedding. I was thinking, What the Hell? I didn't work there, anymore. Although it was awfully nice of him to invite me. Out of kindness, I decided to attend the wedding.

It was a beautiful, sunny Saturday. The wedding was scheduled for noon. I awake early and ready to get the day started. I begged my sister, Les, to attend with me. We were dressing and girl talking. As we drove out farther, we pulled up to a nice exclusive country club. I was so impressed with the surroundings. I had never seen or been exposed to anything like it before.

We were just in time for the reception as we walked in the country club, and it was decorated so beautifully in the color red. I was looking all around for Mister, and my sister and I noticed Dave, his right-hand man in business. He had a comedic personality and always kept us laughing in the office. While we were having conversation, I spotted a few other co-workers. We were having such a great time. We walked outside to see the layout, and there he was with Sharon. They slowly walked toward us.

We exchanged words, and he said, "Glad you guys finally made it. Well, there's plenty of food and drinks, so enjoy yourselves."

The tables had all kinds of delicious food on them, from seafood, salads, pasta, chicken, steak, mashed potatoes, rice, and many other tasty dishes. After being there for about a good hour, my sister and I decided to leave a little earlier, and we said our good-byes.

The next day came, and I received another call. Mister was calling again to thank me and my sister for attending the wedding. He quickly shifted the conversation, asking me out on a dinner date. He wanted to discuss "business." Naturally, I wondered why, since I didn't work for him anymore. What was he talking about? "What kind of business?"

"I have great things in store for you," he said. "I can teach you the ins and the outs of business. That is your college major, after all, right?"

I was fascinated to think that this would finally be my opportunity to advance in the corporate ladder, so I gladly accepted. We hooked up the arrangements for dinner.

Our First Dinner Date

We met up the next day in the evening. I was spending more and more time in the mirror, making sure, that my makeup and hair were flawless. Around seven o'clock, we met at our meeting place. He pulled up in his elegant ride, which was a long, shiny, black Rolls Royce. It was gorgeous, and that was all I knew. He stepped out looking all sharp in a nice black business suit.

He came over to open my car door and said, "Hop in."

I smiled, but at the same time knew and felt that I shouldn't even be here. I was blown away. He drove us to a very fashionable restaurant called Monty's, located in Brentwood, California. As we were seated, I was looking all around the restaurant and at the dinner menu, and I was blown away even more by the prices on it. I ordered Alfredo, a noodle dish, and he ordered Chicken Fried Country Steak with the Mash.

We started eating to the sounds of classical jazz music, and its soothing sound made me relax a little more. We started to converse, and he told me that he was very impressed with me. He wanted to take me under his wing. Leaning forward he said, "I could see in your eyes that you are very driven. When I was around your age, I too had that same drive. Business is not for everyone. It takes a certain kind of person to operate a successful business. I watched you very closely, and you are very different. You're creative, and your style is so smooth. After all, it was my overall decision to hire you. While looking over your job application, I took a liking to your resume. To me, handwriting is an expression. It tells a lot about a person, a story."

I always wrote neat, and very distinctive. I smiled from his compliments. Then he pulled out a small box. "What's this?" I asked.

"It's for you," he said. "Open it."

I handed the gift back to him and said, "I can't accept this." He insisted that I open it, so I did. It was a perfume called Beautiful by Estee Lauder and a sparkling diamond pendant. Again, I told him I couldn't accept it.

He walked over to me then and put the necklace around my neck. "For a very beautiful woman," he said.

Of course, I responded by saying, "Thank you!" I was feeling so special but confused. I always dealt with knuckleheads, who did not know how to treat a woman, so I was feeling very flattered right about now.

Our dinner date ended, and he drove us back to our meeting place. We embraced each other and went our separate ways. The next morning, I woke up knowing that I was only getting myself into something deep, like one of those Lifetime movies.

Later in the day, he called to arrange for a second date. We set up the arrangements, and our date this time was near the beach in Santa Monica, California. How romantic! It was a very nice setting, and again, I was very impressed. Mister was exposing me to a lot of nice sights.

It was a Saturday evening, and my family had taken a quick trip to Las Vegas while I was out of town with my married, ex-boss and having a Margarita cocktail at a night club. I was starting to get more and more relaxed and comfortable with him. He drove us back to our meeting spot, where there was an old truck stop. On the way to the stop, we were listening to the songs of Joe. "I Wanna Know"—this song was, for me, exactly my definition of a man in true love, there to please his woman.

Then Mister started singing the lyrics to me. "Girl, you knock me off my feet... and every time I'm near you I get weak. Nobody has ever made me feel this way... you kiss my lips, and then you take my breath away. I wanna know..." He had a nice singing voice, and then he said to me, "I want to please you in every way, financially and sexually. I want to make you smile and keep you happy."

I was smiling.

Suddenly, he parked the Mercedes. He looked at me, his eyes staring at me, inviting me, calling me to his heart. "What are we doing here?" I asked him.

"It should be evident by now," he responded.

Thoughts started racing quickly through my head, and my emotions were growing stronger and stronger. Then he reached over to me and pulled me closer to him with a strong grip. Suddenly, he was caressing my breast. We started to kiss, and it felt so damn good but crummy at the same time. Then it all came rushing in, and I said, "Stop! I can't do this. You are a married man."

The thought that I was having was is this what he does, on a regular basis with his secretaries? I know men sometimes get bored with their wives and want to spice up their sex life with a side dish, and I didn't want to be his appetizer. I didn't know what his intentions were. After all, he was a man, and one with excessive money and power. I quickly ended the date, feeling good and scared at the same time, and we walked away from each other.

Heading home, I felt things were really escalating out of control. At that moment, I decided to stop seeing him.

～

The following day, he called, and my sister answered the phone. He disguised his voice and said, "Sorry, I dialed the wrong telephone number," and immediately hung up.

I was in the bathroom, washing my face when my sister told me, "Hey, you know that call just now, this man asked for Kaiser Hospital. His voice sounds so familiar though."

My eyes got really big, but I tried not to react in a way that would be too suspicious. "Really," I said. "That's weird."

Mister started blowing me up on my pager. When my sister left the room, I rushed straight to the phone to return his call, and he answered. I told him that he couldn't call me whenever he felt like it. My sister was becoming more and more suspicious. She couldn't find out what was going on with us. She would definitely run and tell my parents if she knew.

"When could I see you again?" he asked.

I had to tell him that there couldn't be me and him anymore. He was married, and that wasn't my thing. But he became very demanding, "I need to see you right away."

I could tell from his voice that he wasn't going to take no for an answer. He insisted that I meet up with him at a nearby park at six thirty in the evening. He wanted to discuss our situation more, in details.

I hesitated but then said, "Okay."

I met him that same day at the park at exactly six thirty. He pulled up in his black Ford work truck, and I got out of my car to get into his car. He handed over to me another gift. "Baby, I miss you," he said. "Open it!"

It was a pretty heart-shaped pendant. "This is for you."

"Thank you" He always knew how to make me feel so special, like a queen. Thoughts of ending the affair were suddenly erased from my memory. We had so much in common, like our strengths and personalities. I was twenty-four years younger, but with an old soul, as he would always say. Actually, it was what made him take notice of me—my grace, my poise.

Most young girls my age didn't carry themselves in the way that I did. I was always very mature for my age. My mentality was tough, which was one of the many reasons why guys my age always had trouble relating to me. They just couldn't keep up with your girl.

Out of the blue, he asked, "Do you want to move out of your parent's house? I think it is time for you to leave the nest."

I was more than ready. I was twenty-five years old, and I always thought, I would move out with my husband or boyfriend. "Of course, I'm ready," I said. I was on the hunt for an apartment. I was looking for the perfect spot, and it was exciting but too scary at the same time. My feelings for Mister were growing stronger and stronger. He was so caring and thoughtful. I hadn't mentioned anything to my parents about what was going on with us. I had to try my best to keep it a secret, which was difficult to do in my house because I came from a close-knit family. I couldn't confide in my sisters because they would only run and tell my parents.

～

He located a nice spot in Harbor City, California and helped me move in and furnished it with very nice, expensive furniture. After we got it all furnished and situated, I invited him over for dinner.

I remembered it like it was just yesterday. I cooked Beef Enchiladas, Refried Beans with a

Green Salad. For dessert, I prepared fruit salad. When I heard a knock on the door, I welcomed him in with a hug and a soft kiss on his lips. He sat as I finished preparing dinner. Then he popped open a bottle of White Zinfandel, and the night was on.

It would be our first time being intimate after all the hugging and kissing we did in the Rolls Royce. After making passionate love, we looked at each other nervously. It was getting late, and he had to get home. I asked myself, how in the hell did I get into this situation? It happened so quickly. I knew it was wrong, and of course, I felt guilty about it all the time. I had grown to love this man. He left around one o'clock in the morning. He had to go to work the next day, and so did I. He dressed and gave me a very passionate kiss, as if the world was ending tomorrow.

I had tears in my eyes. I hated to see him go. I slipped my apartment key in his hand, which was a big move for me. When he left, it only gave me moreand more time to really think about us. My parents did not raise me to be a home-wrecker. It was never my intention. I thought about my parents. How would I've felt if my father had another woman on the side creeping? Mister's words to me were, "You can't break up a marriage that is already easily broken."

He called me as soon as he got home. He wanted to let me know that he made it safely. His actions were so different from that of a man cheating and wanting to keep it a secret. He gave me every phone number he had—his cellular, the house phone number upstairs and the one downstairs, and his business phone number. I thought, when a man wanted to just cheat on his wife but keep her, he would never give his other woman all of his phone numbers.

He called me again the next day, and I told him that we really needed to discuss our situation. I did not want to ever get involved and caught up in a love triangle, which was exactly where this was heading. He agreed, and he picked me up after he got off from work at six thirty in the evening. We had dinner, and we discussed things more again.

"What is this about?" I asked him. "Am I just for sex? Or do we have something more than just that? Let me know so I can grasp this. And please be honest with me!"

He listened and responded, "I am a businessman. I have a lot at stake here. I've acted on my feelings for you. I couldn't help it. I'm just attracted to you. What can I say? Am I happy in my marriage? The answer is no. If I were happy, I wouldn't be here with you right now. So, let's just see where this love goes."

I listened to everything he said. After all the seriousness was out of the way, we finished enjoying the rest of the evening together.

Meanwhile, I was still keeping all of this a huge secret from my parents. They didn't have any idea what was going on with me. I was in love. I walked differently and definitely smiled more. I was so damn happy, the happiest I'd ever been in my life. I never felt like this before. My mother knew something was different about me because I'd been acting so strange lately.

We were getting in the car one day when she asked, "Are you okay? I know when a woman is that happy, a man has to be in the picture somewhere."

I laughed. "Yes, I'm okay. I'm just looking at life in a whole new different perspective."

Now who was I fooling, because I definitely wasn't fooling my Momma. She smiled and said, "Okay," as she looked at me very suspiciously.

Mister ridiculously spoiled me with a nice whip, large amounts of cash, expensive jewelry, stylish clothing, extravagant dinners, and his unselfish and undying love. I often thought I was dreaming. Most women dream of this kind of lifestyle, and I had it all. Financially, I never had any worries. Whatever I needed, I had it. With Mister, I was taken care of pretty well, and with a man like that, any woman couldn't help but fall quicker and deeper in love with him. In my eyes, he wasn't that man I used to work for anymore. He was my boyfriend, my lover. Mister was showing me the meaning of the words "I love you" through his actions, unlike most guys that I would usually date.

Most men like to play so many games. The ones I kept getting always tried to play it with me. I wondered why they couldn't just be truthful like I was. It was so unfair when I was being true, while they were trying to be a player. They always had to get caught up with the game and the lies. But of course, when I found out about it, I never tolerated it. They were dismissed and driven out the door.

Mister, with all the nice things that he was doing for me was able to prove his love to me. The other guys would say, "I love you!" and then turn right around, and hurt me with their constant lies, and cheating. I couldn't believe it. I knew that wasn't true love. How could you say the words, "I love you," and then hurt me?

I questioned myself mentally about it. How could they think that they could play me like a fucking toy? Like I was stupid, or just blind to the facts, and that I couldn't see through all of their bullshit. Don't get it twisted. My momma didn't raise no fool! I wanted a good man, who was deserving of all of my love. One that I felt that I deserved, and that was Mister. Tupac's "Do For Love," was really popular at the time, while Mister was pursing me. It's funny, because the lyrics of the song was straight up him all the way. When I mentioned it to him, he laughs. "What You Won't Do for Love," "You tried everything, but you don't give up." I was always bumping that song in my 1989 Hyundai Excel, sitting on gold star rims. If I can recall, they were tens all day, every day. On my way while driving to work, with the license plate reading 4 Lady Y, on the back of it...Can you picture me rolling? LOL! Reminiscence.

The Attraction

When I became a little older and started to have feelings for the opposite sex, I started to realize that I was intrigued by a man who's a businessman, mainly because of their strength. I loved a strong man who carried a briefcase and dressed in a business suit, a man that could handle his own. Integrity—most businessmen are about it. What I loved about this businessman was his aggressiveness, which was just one of the many reasons why he was very successful. He would never take no for an answer.

He was charismatic, like Billy Dee Williams in Lady Sings the Blues. He could also be as hard as he could be, like a stale cookie. But with me, he was as soft as the filling inside of a twinkie. He was gentle. Whenever we kissed, I could feel the chemistry and the magic, and every time I felt like I was on cloud nine. Every chance we could get we made passionate love. We were each other's drug. I needed him, and he needed me. He wasn't my sugar daddy. For me, it was more than just the money. Otherwise, my love for him would have never lasted a lifetime.

For him, I wasn't just the other woman or a jump-off. It wasn't just about sex, contrary to what most people may think or believe when they see a younger woman with an older man; it is always the first thing being said. But with us, that wasn't the case. We created a strong friendship, a special bond. I gave him a balance between business and his personal life.

Whenever he needed advice, whether it was for business or about family, I was there. He was there for me too. Mister was interested in my dreams and goals. He always stressed to me the importance of education and fulfilling my aspirations. He only wanted the best for me, and he would say this emotionally, with tears forming in his eyes. That was how much he loved and cared for me.

Our love was deep; we were as tight as a hand in a glove. When it came to operating his business, he wasn't ashamed to express his feelings to me. He would tell me how much I meant to him constantly, saying, "Without you, there would be no me." Now that was my definition of a real man. He was a millionaire, who ran a million-dollar company, but with me, he had a whole other side.

The Rendezvous: Part 1

The weekend was here, and we'd both worked so hard. It was time to get away from it all. He booked reservations at the Sheraton in San Diego, California. I had to attend a hair show, so Friday after he got off from work, it was time to hit the 405 freeway. I was packing my things at the last minute when I heard a knock on the door. I opened it. It was him, and we passionately kissed.

"How are you, baby?" he asked.

"I'm well, honey," I replied.

He took my bags. We drove and arrived in San Diego, California, around nine o'clock and pulled up in his sporty black roadster Mercedes.

"Wait! Let the valet attendant open your car door, babe." He demanded royal respect for his woman, and I just loved that about him.

We checked in the hotel then, and it was the perfect getaway for the weekend. Our hotel room was overlooking the ocean. I stepped out on the balcony to the smell of the ocean breeze, and the seagulls were squeaking. The room was lavish too. It was of pure elegance.

After we unpacked and got situated, we watched television. We were lying in the bed together and started to converse. Mister started telling me a story of a millionaire who had all the wealth in the world.

He was so paranoid and unhappy. He did not know whom he could trust. This man was very miserable inside, and he worked diligently. He was a loner and just wasn't a happy person in his life. He only pretended to be happy in front of his family and friends. The man was getting bored with his life because he had experienced it all to the fullest.

I sat, listening, and I couldn't help but wonder. When people use the "friend scenario," they're usually talking about themselves. I listened and listened to the saddest story I'd ever listened to in my life. Once he finished the story, I said, "Wow, that really was a sad story."

Afterward, I excused myself to the restroom, and I was in there a few minutes. When I returned, he reached out to me and turned my face toward him.

"Babe, that friend is me," he said, his eyes teary. "Babe, I am so damn miserable inside." Outside, he pretended to be happy. "When a man or a woman is no longer happy with their spouse and within their marriage, infidelity becomes the inevitable. It's just bound to happen. If he or she sees that person who really catches their eye, it's just going to happen."

He was in a marriage but no longer in a relationship. What did that mean? It meant that he was married but no longer wanted to spend time and enjoy quality moments with his wife. I sympathized with him, for I could understand where he was coming from with it. He only wanted to be happy, to be in love. He was a good father and provider to his family. He felt that he deserved to be happy, and that he shouldn't be feeling guilty for being happy and in love. I felt bad for him.

Here I was, trying to establish my life. I was trying to gain money and a career. For him, money wasn't everything anymore. He only wanted the simple things in life, like a good friend whom he could confide in and trust, who would have his back, and whom he could make good memories with.

My cue was to find out more about the reason why he had to pursue me. First off, he informed me that I reminded him of his first girlfriend. He loved her dearly but he didn't get to marry her because it just didn't work out between them. Also, he pursued me because I stood up to him at work when everyone else just took what he dished out. He loved the fact that I was sassy and had a slick mouth. Actually, it was what made him respect me even more. I was known to have the last word in any argument. It was just me.

"I tried ignoring my feeling for you, but I just couldn't help it," he said. "Whenever I go to bed at night, you are always invading my thoughts, making it more and more difficult for me to go to sleep."

I just listened to him. He watched my demeanor. I was mild-mannered, smart, intelligent, exotic, and very interesting. There was something different about me. I carried myself like I was going to places in life. He loved that about me, and he was definitely correct about all of it. It felt good to hear all this coming from a man of his caliber and status.

I wasn't just a booty call. I had brains, and he admired me for it.

Ending our conversation, he said, "Let's go have dinner."

"Okay," I responded, letting him take the lead.

We ate dinner inside at again another classy restaurant. As the music started to play, he grabbed my hand and said, "May I have this dance, pretty lady?"

"Yes, of course," I replied.

When I was in his presence, I felt like a queen. It was like one of those Cinderella stories. He knew how to charm a woman because he was charming the hell of out me. I felt so safe, so special, so secure with him, and having him in my life only boosted my self-esteem. We danced the night away and later went back to our room for some more loving.

We took a hot, steamy bubble bath, together. He's washing, and caressing my breast with the sponge. He's looking deep into my eyes. We kiss passionately. After, he dried the dripping water from my body, from head to my toes. He picked me up, lying me on the bed. He rubs and massages baby oil all over my body, with his masculine hands. He took his time to relax my stressed body. He always made sure he took care of me in a special way. The cherry on the top was the intimacy. It wouldn't take me too much longer, after all of that. He knew exactly what to do. Making me feel like a woman, I'm exploding…

We made love, until the sun came up. We looked at each other both so, in love. We were so happy.

We awoke the next morning in each other's arms. We were ready to get the day started, and the plan was to go to the San Diego Zoo. We walked all around the park, took tours, and just let loose. Around him, I could be my true self, and he could be himself with me. The people who encountered us would smile, as if they'd seen two people who truly loved each other. Of course, we always received a lot of attention. Love is love, and that was what we shared. Age didn't matter to us; it's just a number.

It was a long and exhausting day for the both of us, so we checked back into our hotel room.

The next day was a big day for me; it would be a huge event. I would be attending The International Hair Show, and there were people from all over the world who would also be at this event. The next day was Sunday. At the hair show, there were so many hair designers competing, all showing off their creative talents and skills. I attended a few classes and purchased some hair products that I needed while Mister walked around the auditorium, sightseeing.

The show was over about five o'clock, and we somehow got lost from one another. There were so many people there. I searched and searched, but I couldn't locate Mister. I went to make a phone call at the pay phone in hopes that he would soon show up. I was probably on the telephone for about five minutes, talking to my youngest sister when I saw him walking toward me. He appeared to be a little disgruntled. Once he got closer, I hung up the telephone.

When he approached me; he was furious. What in the hell was his problem?

"Who was that?" he asked.

"Are you serious?" I answered.

I guessed he thought I was talking to another man. I had never seen him act like this before. He was extremely jealous, and his insecurities came probably because he had a friend, Earl, who was putting all kinds of bad thoughts in his head and salt in his ears, saying stuff like, "Man, that young tenderoni is just playing you. I bet you right now, at this very moment she is in the bed withanother dude. A younger dude." He was making me out to be some kind of a gold digger. He wanted Mister to believe that I was all about the money.

Of course, it wasn't just about the money. Love was involved for me too. Over a period of time, he found out that I had always been faithful to him with my love and my heart. His jealousy was kind of cute to me though.

We got into our very first argument. What I was upset about was the thought that he didn't trust me. I mean, look at the situation: he had a wife, and I wasn't proud about it. He assured me that if our relationship was good, if we were truly happy in ours despite the arguments and ups and downs, he would finally make the decision to leave his wife.

I concentrated on all the things that I needed to focus on, like my career. I was trying to establish myself as a cosmetologist. I had been independent all of my life, and I still wanted that independence. I wanted to be able to say that I can be successful too. It was time for us to go back home. We went back to our hotel room for our final checkout.

I felt he only wanted to pick an argument with me because of his guilt. Our fun was over. He somehow had to mentally prepare himself for work and Sharon. It was silent on the trip home. As we exited the 110 freeway, he apologized to me. I wasn't happy with the fact of him having a wife. But for me, I had to be available at all times. This was not supposed to be in our deal.

We both knew what we were getting ourselves into. I had trouble accepting the fact that he had to go home, leave me, only to carry on a game of charades with his Sharon. He would stay some late nights and drove forty-five minutes to go back home to his wife. He dealt with a woman whom he no longer saw as a lover but only as a business partner. I knew he had to be catching a lot of slack for it and for his constant whereabouts.

We pulled up to my apartment. He walked me to my door, and he stayed a few minutes before he made his way home. We always had a great time in each other's company. It was always difficult saying good-bye when it came time for him to go. It was time for me to prepare myself for my exciting week ahead. I took a hot bubble bath, reflecting back on life and this crazy situation I was in. I was still keeping this a secret from my family. I was lying like a rug, and I was using my friends to cover up my whereabouts. I didn't like it, but the timing wasn't exactly perfect to tell them.

The Secret Is Out

In the beginning of our courtship, if we couldn't be together, we were always having long conversations on the telephone. We could talk up a storm. He later bought me a cellular phone so he could keep track on me at all times. We talked so much, and it started to raise suspicions—and eyebrow —on the part of his wife.

She received the telephone bill, which was twenty pages long, and on it was my cell phone number. Mister lived in a long-distance area code. We forgot that phone records would track every time and conversation, and of course, she would be very curious to find out who he was talking to so much. The phone rang twice. I picked up and heard an echo, and I thought it was the children playing tricks again, downstairs on the intercom.

"Who is this?" A female voice that I didn't recognize said, and before I knew it my name slipped out.

"Yvette?" "Yes," I replied.

She said, "Okay," and immediately hung up the telephone.

And then I thought, Oh my gosh! It's wifey! I was completely caught off guard. I quickly called Mister, and he answered, sounding exhausted from a long day at work. "She knows," I said.

"What? Who?" "Sharon!" "Don't worry about it, baby," he said. "I will handle it when I get home."

I tried not to worry, but I knew I was going to have to deal with the wrath of it all. I started pacing back and forth. What am I going to say to her when she calls? I tried to settle myself down. I knew she was going to call me back so she could find out what the hell was going on with me and Mister that night, I tossed and turned. What am I going to say to her?

The next morning, I awoke to the phone ringing around seven thirty.

"Hello, Yvette! I'm calling to find out what the hell is going on with you and my husband." I thought, are you serious? Even though she picked up the telephone to initiate the first call for him, especially knowing the circumstances. Now what woman would do that for her man? If that were my husband, I would never have called another woman for him. He had already told her that he had only been pretending for many years and was tired of it. He wasn't going to do it anymore. He was on my side.

She was shocked, and I was shocked too. I never would have thought that Mister would jeopardize his marriage for us, for what we had. But he did. It only let me know that my feelings were not in this alone. Mister gave his wife an ultimatum. If he couldn't be with me, then he would want a divorce. He didn't want to be married to her anymore.

Of course, she wasn't happy about it, but she agreed to the arrangement. She gave him permission to continue on with our relationship, as long as we were only friends. She was in total denial, I guessed, because Mister and I were way past the friendship status. I started to realize how deep his love was for me. We were caught up in a love triangle, with Mister in the middle and his wife pulling his left arm and trying so desperately to hang onto their thirty-something-year marriage, while I was pulling his right arm, trying to hold onto the man whom I had fallen so deeply in love with.

He was like a toy, and Sharon and I were like two children tugging back and forth, saying, "He's mine." I wasn't going to let go, and neither was she. This was the kind of arrangement we had. We continued on in our relationship. Mister's secret was off of his shoulders, but for me, I was plagued by deceit. In the beginning of our relationship, I felt so damn guilty, and Mister always assured me that I didn't do anything wrong. I couldn't help it because he fell in love with me the moment he first saw me.

He confided to me once, "I would have chased after you until I got that yes."

I didn't want to be a homewrecker, but that wasn't exactly the case. His kids were in their twenties and already grown-ups. His words always consoled me. The lies to my family, the shame, they just haunted me. It even got to a point that I just wasn't comfortable with hiding it anymore. "We can't continue on like this," I said to him. "I have to let my parents know what is going on with us."

"What!" he said. "Your parents are going to kill me!" It had to be this way if he wanted to continue a relationship with me, so he finally agreed on having a meeting with my parents.

The Rendezvous: Part 2

Our second getaway trip was the most memorable. It was more exciting to me than the first trip to San Diego. Instead of making the four-and-a-half-hour drive and dealing with that California West Coast traffic, we took a flight. He booked reservations with Southwest Airlines, and we left on a Friday afternoon around one o'clock. I was so damn nervous inside. I hadn't flown in an airplane since that trip to Hawaii in 1989. My heart was beating so rapidly once we hit the airport.

"Babe, it's going to be all right. You are with me. If we crash, we die together," Mister told me with a huge smile on his face.

He didn't know it, but those words really scared the hell out of me. We were together, but I wasn't ready to die. I breathed in and then exhaled. We checked our luggage in at the check-in desk. We had to wait about thirty minutes until we were able to board our plane and find our seats, and my heart was beating even harder and faster. Once everyone was aboard, the pilot cleared us for takeoff. I closed my eyes, rested my head on his shoulder, grabbed Mister's hand so tightly, and prayed.

Within forty-five minutes, we were touching down. "We have just arrived in Las Vegas, Nevada. The weather is fair, seventy degrees. Have fun!" the pilot billowed on the intercom.

We exited the airplane and proceeded to the terminal. We arrived safely, thank God! It was time to locate some wheels; we rented a smooth sports car. Mister drove us to his Vegas condo. He inserted the key in the keyhole, and we went inside.

"Wow! Very impressive!" I said. Indeed, this crib was pure luxury. Mister's condo was something right out of MTV Cribs Celebrity Edition.

The Meet with the Parents

I hooked up the arrangements for Mister to meet with my parents, and it all went down on a Saturday afternoon at one of my favorite Mexican food restaurants, El Torito. I was so nervous inside. What are my parents going to think and say? He was married, that was a first strike. I swung out again, second strike. He was twenty-four years older than me, particularly the same age as my father. I couldn't keep our love a secret any longer. I had been acting so damn strange—happy, sad, all kinds of emotions—and this man was the reason for it. It was time for my confession.

Although my parents already had their suspicion, they could see that I was very much in love. They just didn't know who with. I had, as they call it, the "Glow." Mister came over to pick me up from my apartment. He was looking so handsome with his hair neatly groomed. He was wearing Cool Water cologne, a nice-smelling fragrance with a masculine scent. He was wearing a dark blue suit, with some black, shiny Stacy Adams dress shoes. He was looking sharp, indeed.

I greeted him with a juicy kiss. We were on our way to meet up with my parents. We arrived about twelve o'clock noon at the restaurant and showed up a little earlier before my parents. We were seated at the table. I tried to make Mister relax, but he was so damn nervous. And he had every right to be. This was a hell of a situation to be in. I glanced to the right, looking out of the window, and I could see my parents driving into the parking lot. I looked and turned to him with a smile on my face, and he smiled back with a nervous look on his. They parked their car and started to walk towards us.

I waved at them with my hand. Once they reached us, we exchanged smiles and hellos.

I immediately introduced Mister to them. We had the deepest conversation ever. My boyfriend explained what his attraction to me was and went on to say that he had only good intentions for me. He only wanted the best out of life for me. Although he was married, he knew that if our love was going to continue, he was going to have to make a choice.

"What the hell is going on here, man?" my father asked. "You are married. You can't be with two women at the same time. You know what that makes you? A damn cheater, not to mention a polygamist.

"Look, I'm sorry for what I have done! It wasn't my intention to fall in love with your daughter. My heart did something I had no control over. She is smart, attractive, and funny," Mister said.

My parents weren't too thrilled of the facts. They weren't upset about the age difference, only of the fact that he was a married man. Their only concern was me, their oldest daughter. They had to look out for my best interest. They didn't want me to get caught up in a love triangle because they were afraid that that would hurt me and possibly destroy me. But it was way too late for that now. I was already caught up in his love. There were so many questions. For one, they wondered where all the jewelry, the money, the apartment, and the car were all coming from. I was only working a part-time job and certainly couldn't pull in that kind of dough.

It all finally started to make sense to them, as if all the pieces to the puzzle came together. My father became livid with the conversation, while my mother listened and tried to make sense of it all. Suddenly, my father knocked over his drink with anger.

"C'mon, honey! Let's go. I have heard about enough of this," he said, and, together with my mother, stormed out of the restaurant.

The truth was out for us. No more secrets and no more lies. I didn't have to feel guilty anymore. They just couldn't understand us. How could we turn around now? We were both in love so deep and were both caught up. It tore me up inside because every woman wanted the blessing of their parents when they finally found that special man, and it was evident that it wasn't happening here, especially in this kind of situation. Anyway, all that mattered to me was that the truth was finally out. I loved him, and he loved me. It was all that really mattered to me. Mister and I still kept spending every chance we could to be together.

Someone Has to Lose

The one thing about being in a love triangle was that someone was going to get hurt in the situation. Sharon and I instantly became adversaries because we shared a common interest—Mister Someone had to lose. There was no happy outcome for one person, and I didn't want to be that person. I totally risked myself for him.

In the beginning of our relationship, I was extremely cautious and skeptical of his love for me. I had many insecurities floating around in my head, like knowing that he had to be intimate with his wife. Now that hurt. Could I believe what he was telling me about their sex life? Was it really true when he said that when he touched her, it just didn't feel the same anymore, because the love was gone?

I didn't know what to believe at first, especially in this kind of situation. What if this man would get bored and tired of me? Will he discard me like he did to his wife? Or will he want to go back to her and pretend that the love we had never even existed. I couldn't accept it. This was what my parents constantly worried about the most for me. Mister's feelings for me could change anytime. If they ever would, I could become a violent, crazy stalker kind of woman. Kidding aside, I had never stalked anybody before in my life, but with him, I probably just would.

The Transformation

Mister transformed me into his Phenomenal Woman. I hated wearing high heels, but I did for him. I started wearing more dresses and less pants. I showed off my legs more; he called them thick and sexy.

It was an early Saturday morning when he picked me up and took me to Macy's for a complete makeover. He purchased Shiseido makeup for me, foundation, eye shadow, eye liner, among others. I had worn makeup many times before but only on special occasions. When I was younger, my mother always tried convincing me to wear full makeup every day. But to me, I was always like, what for? I didn't have that special man in my life. Instead of thinking of doing it for myself first and foremost, I would always ask, who was I trying to impress?

I guessed I wasn't ready to make that change. I realized at that moment that I was maturing into a woman phenomenally. This man made me want to. My attitude was so different from before. I had been hanging around with him. I walked with grace and confidence. I picked up on how to talk to people so they would respect and take me seriously. I demanded respect and damn well was going to receive it. It is true what they say, that once you hang out or spend a lot of time with someone, you start to develop their ways and actions.

I did, and it wasn't negative though. It was all positive. I looked up to him, admired him, and was inspired by him. I transformed into the Phenomenal Woman that he wanted me to be. It was a transformation but only for the better. Later on, we went shopping for clothes. The lesson of that day was "dress for success," and I remembered him saying to me, "When you look good, you feel good about yourself. You'll do your best." That is absolutely true.

My 27th Birthday

It was my 27th birthday. Every time my birthday came around, I was always like a little girl. Mister picked me up from my apartment and sang "Happy Birthday to You." He then handed me an envelope, which contained a card. The card had a cute little brown bear on it and a comical message, and it read:

> *Whoever opens this card will get a big birthday hug! I was hoping it would be you!*

I smiled and kissed him for it. Inside the card were hundred-dollar bills after hundred-dollar bills. It totaled out to be about one thousand dollars.

Smiling, he said, "Go shopping, baby!" It was always his motto.

We drove to our spot again—San Diego, California— and the weather was like eighty degrees. We watched a movie, and afterward went to the indoor/ outdoor shopping mall. We walked into a store called BCBG. This store was off the chain. It was no joke; it was also very expensive. I walked around, checking out the clothes until I came across this bad black silk business suit. It cost $616.38. Mister was looking at clothes on the other side of the store.

He saw me looking at him and walked over and asked, "Babe, you see anything you like?"

"I sure do. I bought a suit."

And then we were off to a surprise in Pasadena, California. The surprise was actually a live play at the Pasadena Playhouse. The theme of the play was Cab Calloway, and it was my first live play ever. We received a lot of extra attention that night, particularly from two older ladies. I was dressed in a pretty blue dress with a wraparound shawl that went around my neck. I felt like a million bucks. I was feeling very pretty, like a princess, and Mister was looking all fly in a dark blue suit, his favorite color. He was my prince, and the two ladies could see how strong our love was.

They even walked up to us and said, "You two make a very nice-looking couple."

We smiled and said, "Thank you!"

We had so much fun that night.

Trouble with My Best Friends

My love affair with Mister did make my life a whole lot easier when it came to my finances. He always had my back, and I didn't have to worry about my bills, or if I had a problem with my car, he was there to fix it. I had a stress-free life, with no worries for money or anything else. My new lifestyle had changed me to some degree, but not to a point where I became stank, with a nasty attitude. I stayed grounded and true to myself because I was taught never to forget where I came from. Just as easy as it was for me to go up the ladder, I could always come quickly tumbling down.

Mister gave me a new outlook in life. Hanging around a million-dollar man also gave me a million ideas of what I wanted to do with my career. The new change in me was all for the good. They say change is good because it means that you are maturing and advancing to another level of your life. My perspective on life was different than it had been before, especially when it came to comparing of lifestyles with a lot of my friends. I had bigger and better dreams for success. I had a vision. Our friendship shifted only because they weren't on that same level of thinking as I was.

Mister had shared to me that when he became successful, he really had to be very careful of the company he kept. Envy and jealousy were always lurking his way.

They didn't understand him. For what people don't understand, they fear, and this made a whole lot of sense to me. This was the reason why he became a loner. He didn't know whom he could trust, but he trusted me. He confided in me with his many personal and business matters, some that I will never and can't reveal.

Our love affair brought a sense of joy to my heart, although it also brought some turbulence along the way. The relationship between me and my sister Les, who brought me the referral pink card and got it all started, became rough and bumpy. Because of my new lifestyle, my sister lost all respect for me. She couldn't comprehend why, and my parents couldn't either. It was something I never planned on doing. Sometimes in life, things just happen and you absolutely have no control over them.

I didn't wear slutty clothing around him to entice him to want me, or flirt with him so he would want to become involved with me. I always kept respect for myself and his wife, so why did I turn out to be the villain in all of this? Love is like that sometimes. We have no control over who we fall in love with. When you are in love, no one can tell you anything. Your head is so far in the clouds. Love can sometime make you blind to the real facts.

The main fact was that I never had to worry about being taken advantage of by him. Why? Because of a four-letter word—LOVE! We loved each other unconditionally, and that was all there was to understand.

My family just saw it for the sin that it was, and my sister and I argued a lot more. She would say to me, "How would you like it if your husband did that to you? How could you do that to her?" I understood what she meant by it, but at the same time I also understood that what you don't allow could and would never happen.

Sharon knew it, and yet allowed it, so it wasn't my fault. My sister and I were very close, and this brought a wedge between us. Sometimes, I questioned her judgment of me. I wondered if she was really upset because of what I was doing, or because I was being showered with so many luxuries. Every time I received a new gift, whether it was jewelry or cash, I always had to deal with her snappy attitude. It hurt my feelings to know that our close bond was dissipating.

Sometimes you really can't satisfy everyone. I had to make myself happy, and Mister was doing it for me. My youngest sister Jay, whom I was on the telephone with when Mister had a hissy fit, could have cared less about all of it. At the time, she was really young and very popular with her friends. My sister was always in the streets. She never really got too caught up in my life. She just kept hers moving.

My Storm

I was mesmerized by his love. It was taking me higher and higher to ecstasy. I also spent a lot of time listening to Aaliyah's "Age Ain't Nothing but a Number." Isn't that the truth? I never thought I would fall so deep in love with a man twice my age, but it happened. I felt secure with him, and I wasn't afraid of getting my feelings hurt by him. Mister loved me, and when we weren't together, he always evaded my mind.

While juggling school and work, I was always dreaming of him and the next time that I would see him. It was so difficult trying to stay focused in school. It seemed to become a chore. Many times, Mister came to visit me on his lunch breaks. We were touching, and kissing. The lovemaking was so intense and to the point. He was gentle and soft in his strokes. He knew how to get me off. What I loved most about dealing with an older man was that I didn't have to show or teach him anything when it came to sex.

But for some strange reason, the feeling wasn't amazing this time; it was hurting. My body was feeling so uncomfortable—so uncomfortable that I had to say, "Stop!"

"What's wrong?" he asked.

"Babe, it actually hurts."

I noticed that this was happening every time we made love. It was getting worse and worse. I eventually had to schedule an appointment with my OB-GYN to find out what was going on with me. A week later, I was extremely nervous; it was my appointment.

The gynecologist put cold clear gel on my stomach as I was lying there with uncertainty. She started to roll the wand back and forth slowly on my belly. I didn't need to hear any kind of negative news that would change the happiness that I was having in my life. Another week passed on, and the results were in. I was diagnosed to have fibroid tumors.

When I found out the results of my ultrasound, Mister got off from work early and rushed to my side. When I opened the door, I broke down crying on him. I was scared to death.

"Baby, everything is going to be all right," he consoled.

A dark cloud was forming over me. Karma seemed to be coming right back around and biting me. Karma could be a bitch too. Was I being punished? I didn't know. All I knew was that I felt sick all of the time, from the moment my feet would hit the floor to the time I would be going to bed. I couldn't hold down food, causing me to lose a lot of weight. I weighed about 135 pounds, but it dropped to about 120 pounds.

I remembered one day I was sitting in my car on my lunch break, eating my lunch, I started to feel extremely nauseous all of a sudden. Doctors later informed me that I needed to have immediate surgery. I really had no choice; there was no exception. I had to have a procedure called myomectomy. With this procedure, doctors had to remove tumors that developed in the walls of a woman's uterus. I was mortified—no, scared to death—by the idea of a surgery. I didn't want this to affect my chances of ever becoming a mother one day.

I had a major decision to make, and I came to a conclusion: it was surgery time. The night before, sleep didn't come easy to me. I tossed and turned, rolling in my bed back and forth. I was up at four o'clock in the morning; the rooster wasn't even awake. I was trying to get myself mentally prepared.

I arrived at the hospital around five o'clock, and it was early as hell. As the nurses were prepping me for surgery, I immediately started praying to God. Please let the surgery go well. Please let the doctors do what they need to in order for me to feel better again. And then I felt like slipping out of my consciousness until the anesthesia knocked me out, like a boxer knocking out his opponent, with no conscious feeling of what was going to happen or what was going on around me.

The surgery was about forty-five minutes long, and I awoke to the most excruciating pain ever. "Damn it! Give me some pain drugs." I screamed out to the nurses. "I need it, hurry please!"

I was crying uncontrollably. I was in so much pain, and all because of the staples piercing through my stomach in order for my enormous belly incision to heal. The surgery was a complete success. The doctors were able to remove multiple tumors from my uterus (there was even one fibroid that was as big as a grapefruit).

My boyfriend quickly rushed to my bedside. My entire family was there too. There was a little tension in the air. You could see and feel it. But my family was finally starting to really realize how much Mister cared for me. My mother and father started to respect him more.

Mister was assisting me and walking me to the restroom. We were taking just baby steps at a time. He was combing my hair and wiping my face. He was there trying to make me feel as comfortable as I could. I didn't want him seeing me in that kind of shape, with no makeup on and my hair a total mess. But when someone truly loves you, that's what it's all about. I didn't have to be embarrassed about it. My only focus now was my recovery.

A few weeks went by, and I was recovering extremely well. I was out of commission for about six weeks. At this time, there could be no sexual relationship for us. Of course, I started to worry about Mister I couldn't sexually satisfy him right now, but then he assured me that he wasn't having sex anymore with his wife. I couldn't worry. I had to concentrate only on myself.

Back to life, back to reality.

I thought more and more about having a baby—

his baby—because doctors had warned me that the fibroids could come back again anytime. I really wanted a child but only with a man that loved me and could support us all. I never desired to have a baby with a man who wasn't worthy of me and my love. I never wanted a lot of children; just one child so I could say that I was a mother.

At first, I was afraid of getting pregnant, especially in this situation, but then Mister made it loud and clear to me that it would be impossible anyway. When I heard the word "impossible," I asked him, "What do you mean?"

"I had a vasectomy."

When Mister was in his early thirties, when he had his vasectomy, he was no longer able to have children, unless he would have it reversed. But he didn't want to have children anymore. It was totally out of the question for him, for us.

He was in his fifties. I tried to be understanding about it, but this is where I was in my life right now. Because of our age difference, we were at two different places, stages in our lives. We started to disagree, and have more and more arguments. But having a child was my main focus. Until one day, Mister surprised me with the cutest little toy poodle. I named him "Pepper." He was such a cutie. He was black with curly, long, fluffy ears. He had the cutest puppy brown eyes.

Mister thought it would be the next best thing to a baby. Pepper pacified me for a while. Again, it became regular conversation of ours. I had it all, except motherhood. I wanted to have his baby. I wanted to hear the word momma coming from my baby's mouth, my creation.

But at the same time, it wouldn't be complete for me, and I couldn't be satisfied with me until I know who I was as a woman. I needed to find my purpose in this life. Without finding me, how could I make my child happy? If I wasn't completely happy, what could I teach my baby? I couldn't truly be happy without finding my own success. So, I kept searching for me. Who am I?

Sharon knew the truth about us. She gave Mister approval to be with me. In her world, she wanted to believe that things were all good in their marriage. She didn't want a divorce, because materialistically there was so much involved. The fact that Mister was in love with me, a younger woman was humiliating for her, and plus it would have been the talk of the town. So, she kept quiet, and went along with it all. She let us be together. She knew that he didn't love her like that, anymore.

My Proposal

It's Christmas time, the year 2002.

His work schedule became more, and busier. For he of course, had to cater to his many customers. He had several big accounts, and state contracts.

Christmas was my most favorite holiday. Buying gifts, and sharing the love. What a special time, for us. Although, he was so busy. He did take the time out to drop off, a huge Christmas present. On Christmas Eve with a big Kool-Aid smile.

"Don't open it, until tomorrow!"

I assured him that I would wait. I was excited to find out what was inside this box. I shook it, wandering. I awoke the next morning, early. I opened my gifts with my family. I opened all the other gifts, first.

Then it came time to open, Mister's. It was wrapped in a box, with the prettiest Christmas wrapping paper. When I opened the medium size box, there was another smaller box, inside. What a joker. It appears to be a small, black jewelry box. There was a note attached to it. It read *'please don't open me until 7:30 p.m. At that time, I can be there with you.'*

I had to be patient. I had to wait, until later that evening. What could it be that he had to be here with me?

He shows up, around 7:15p.m. I was so excited to find out what was inside the small box. I opened it with excitement. It was beautiful! A 1 1/2 carat engagement ring, with diamonds glistening, on both sides of it. The ring was nothing of the same. I had tried on when we went shopping together at the South Coast Plaza Mall. He was in a hell of position with me. He wanted to keep me, and he knew that I was becoming more, and more restless. Frustrated really, I wanted to be the one he woke up to every day, in the morning. Commitment, is what I wanted.

This is how, he proposed to me. "But how could we be engaged, you haven't even divorced yet?"

"Uhm…" He said, "We are not the only ones, in this kind of situation. Trust me. People do this all the time. I love you, and I'm working on it."

It was going to take some time. Because he, and wifey were business partners. There was so much at stake here. So, I accepted it. Honestly, I felt married to him already. We were that close with our special bond. Only thing is, I didn't have the legal papers to prove it. I had everything else, though. His time, his love, and his money. In which he always made it a point, that his money was mine. I was the happiest woman in the world. He put the ring on my ring finger, and I was showing it off to all my friends and family. My family knew I loved him, deep down inside of their hearts, they knew he loved me too.

What man would subject himself to meet his young girlfriend's parents, knowing that he was married? It didn't matter to us about our age difference. It didn't matter to my parents, either. It was just the fact that he was a married man. But he wasn't happily married.

One day he sat down with me and he explained everything in depth to me about his finances. What would happen if he decided to make that decision to leave sooner. First off, he wouldn't be able to provide the best lifestyle for me. It would have been a good life, but not the best life of living it to the fullest. Because a judge would grant Sharon, most of the financials. Based on the time, she put in within their marriage. There was no prenuptial agreement.

She would win big in this. He wanted to give me more than that. Plus, the fact he needed her to assist him, with operating the business. "So, we'll wait. When I retire, we are going to get married."

I didn't trip on it. He was very close to retiring, so I trusted his integrity. Because he was that kind of man. Everything that he ever told me, he always did it. Like when I was in the hospital for surgery with the fibroids. I was off from work for two months. The bills started piling up and he told me, "Not to worry."

Sure enough, he handed me an envelope with one-hundred-dollar bills, after one-hundred-dollar bills, or the time my car broke down, and he bought me a new one. He was good to me. That's how it was. Our relationship was heading in a more definite, and positive direction.

Here Comes Another Storm

It was Sunday, with clear blue skies. My thoughts were lost in the clouds. The two-hour drive was relaxing. I was with him, and he was with me. We talked, shared some laughs, and arrived to the smell of beach in the air. This time, we were in Santa Barbara, California. We walked along the coast and did some sightseeing. For lunch, we ate delicious seafood at one of the restaurants on the beach. After lunch, we walked hand in hand along the shore. He didn't like the sand, but I convinced him to take his shoes off, as I did too.

"Ugh. This is gross. But I will do it for you."

We walked along the beach, with the sand on our toes. The breeze was also blowing through our hair. I was still so in love with him, but again, the thought of having his baby kept running in my head. To him, I was like a broken record about this. As we were walking in the sand, I asked him about it again.

He smiled and said, "So a baby, that would really make you happy, huh? Me too." He would often kid around with the waiters at the restaurant, telling them all that I was having his baby. He was finally beginning to come around to the idea of having a baby. "If I were to have a baby with you the second time around, I would be a better father, because I would be able to devote more time and focus on my family. I wouldn't be paper chasing," he said.

He was good in his career and very close to retiring. We also came to a major decision we both agreed on. We were happy, and he set up a doctor's appointment so he could have his vasectomy reversed. It wasn't a hundred percent guarantee. What was more important to me was that he cared that much for me to even consider it. He went ahead with the process though, and it was worth trying. We were both so excited.

First, he had to get to his regular medical doctor. The doctors wanted to make sure that his overall health was all good. They ran several tests, including checking for sugar diabetes, high blood pressure, and PSA men health test. All we needed to do now was wait. We waited patiently for the results.

As we were waiting for the results to come in, Mister received a call—one that would change his life forever. Mister received news that his father was in the hospital and was extremely ill. His father wasn't present in his life earlier on. They reconnected and developed this amazing father-and-son bond in the later years of his life. Mister was around thirty-five years old when they rekindled their relationship. I saw a strong man turn sensitive. He truly loved his father with all his heart.

When he confided in me, I was so sympathetic to him and his feelings. Any conversation about anything else was on pause. I wanted to be there for him when he had to go out of town, to Alabama, but I couldn't. He would be away for about five days. I missed him to death, but I kept myself busy with my work. He was there for his father at his bedside in the hospital, and they were reminiscing about old times. For Mister these were the precious times that he would always remember.

Then business became demanding, and Mister had to get back quickly. A lot of business problems were going on. When he returned, his father had passed away. I was sad for him, so I gave him the space he needed to grieve. I did what I needed to do and let him grieve. Losing a loved one really makes you think about how precious life and family are.

As time passed on, he checked back into life and its reality, but the second storm to come. The results and his medical report were in the mail. He needed to come in for his results, and I thought, this couldn't be good. On that day, he received disturbing bad news. He was diagnosed with Stage 1 Prostate Cancer. Whoa!

The doctors recommended immediately that he start chemotherapy and radiation treatments. He was devastated, of course, and he said to himself, "How could this be? I ate healthy, exercised, and took really good care of myself over the years. I knew stress could be a demon, but damn!" He was definitely stressed. He had plenty of drama going on in his life.

For twenty-something years, he was running a very successful business and had a love triangle going on with me and Sharon. He was being where he didn't want to be and worried about where he couldn't be. It, of course, was an extreme overload. I knew this was what made him ill. I knew!

Then there was some distance between us. I hadn't spoken to Mister in a few days. I worried, so I called his cell phone, but there was no answer. It went straight to his voicemail. I called the house numbers, and again there was no answer. I did the two-ring code that we established, although Sharon said that when I wanted to talk to him, it was all right for me to call the house. I never felt too comfortable with that, so I would always let the phone ring twice and hang up so he could call me back. But he didn't call me back, and I wondered hard.

I knew his father had just passed away, and I gave him enough time to grieve. In myheart, I felt something else was going on with him other than the loss of his father. I didn't know for sure, so I left several messages on his voicemail, "Please call me. I miss you."

He finally called me back.

"What's wrong?" I asked him.

"Babe, I have been distant to you. I know, I'm sorry. I have been thinking about us a lot."

I interrupted him, "Okay. What is going on with you? Please, tell me."

"I don't know how to tell you this. I don't want to hurt you and scare you. It's not good. You're going to have to brace yourself for the news I'm about to give you."

I felt my stomach lurching and my nerves cringing. "What, babe? What!"

"I have been diagnosed with Stage 1 Prostate Cancer." My heart hit the floor. "What?" He went on to say that the doctors said that we should be thankful for inquiring about the vasectomy reversal. Otherwise, they probably would have caught it too late.

I tried to process the news. I wanted to break down like a baby and cry. He was afraid, I was afraid. "Babe, I'm terrified. I can't leave you. I'm not ready to. I'm fighting for this, fighting for us," he said.

The thought of him being erased from my life was never in the equation. I couldn't fathom it. Blind, I couldn't see the reality that was before me. I had to be strong for Mister. I had to show him that everything was going to be all right. The Leo lion in me had to kick in, and quick. I spent a lot of time doing research about Prostate Cancer.

I encouraged him and prayed for him. We were going to get through this tragedy together. I was faithful and always by his side. We had to be optimistic for this fight. He scheduled appointments to the doctor twice a week for chemotherapy and radiation treatments.

The first procedure was for him to stop wearing chemicals in his hair. He hated this because he loved his texturizer. So did I, but he had to do what he had to do. He went back and forth to the hospital. In the very beginning, I watched a warrior fighting for his life. Over a period of time, the treatments made him feel horrible. It was going to take some time getting used to, because his body had to become immune to the treatments. He described the feeling as something as if weights were pulling his body down. He was extremely tired and always at a loss for energy.

Later on, he didn't feel handsome and strong anymore.

I assured him that he looked handsome to me, even better than before, in fact, because he was a fighter. His family was not aware of his medical condition, and he wanted to keep it that way. He wanted to keep it a secret.

I couldn't believe it. "How could you do that?" I asked.

"This would destroy my kids," he said. "I don't want to hurt them."

He had a son, who was a cosmetic dentist, and a daughter, who was a good attorney, and he loved them both dearly. I kept telling him that he needed to tell them, so he could have the support of everyone. We argued about it. Later, he finally agreed with me. The man could be so damn stubborn!

Months into his treatment, it was really starting to take a toll on his body. His complexion became darker, and his weight fluctuated up and down. He was complaining more and more to me. I sympathized for him, and I couldn't imagine the pain he was going through. On top of it all, he had the pressures of operating the company. It was way too much stress to endure.

AGE AIN'T NOTHING BUT A NUMBER

I wanted to make it all better for him, but I couldn't. I told my family about Mister's cancer diagnosis, and for the second time in my life, I was afraid. I needed my family's support. They gave me the strength that I needed to be there for him. We kept a positive attitude for his recovery. As time progressed, he became a little more adjusted to his treatments. We went on with our lives, just trying to block the cancer out of our minds.

~

It was May 24, 2004. Musician Prince was in town. I had never seen Prince live in concert before. Mister loved Prince too, so we went to see him perform in Anaheim, California.

I waited for him to get

off from work at six thirty in the evening. He was tired, but he still wanted to take me. Before he had gotten sick, he always spoke about taking me to see Prince. We arrived in the venue, and we waited in line to pick up our tickets. I couldn't believe that I was finally going to see Prince. I was in my thirties by then, and I had been a huge fan since I was fourteen. We located our seats and enjoyed the magnificent sound of music.

Mister excused himself to the restroom and was gone for about fifteen-minutes. When he returned, he realized that he didn't have his bag. "Hey, babe, where's my bag?"

"I thought you took it with you," I said.

"Oh, my goodness! My bag has a thousand

dollars in cash in it, all my credit cards, identification, and some important business documents." He became very jittery in his seat.

The concert was slowly wrapping up. We left a little, earlier so we could locate his black bag. He searched and searched the restroom, but there was no bag in sight.

"Let's go to Lost and Found," I told him. "Maybe it's there."

He agreed, and we walked quickly to the Lost and Found booth.

Once we were there, a lady said, "Can I help you?"

"Yes, I'm looking for a black man bag. Is it here?"

"No." the lady said.

He had a frantic look in his eyes. Mister noticed several items covering up other items, so he asked." Can you remove the jackets?"

The lady removed the other items, and there was the black bag. He was ecstatic, as I would be too. He immediately looked inside his bag to make sure that everything was still in it. It was all good. I was so happy he located his bag. I didn't want him worrying at all. Stress was definitely not good for him right now.

Also, it would have been a long, disappointing ride on the way home if he hadn't been able to find it.

We had a fun night, with a twist of scare. He never took no for an answer or gave up. He was a fighter, indeed, and that was what he taught me.

"There is always a way to get things done. You just have to be consistent and persistent. You must use your brain. You have to be a driving force." These were his exact words.

It was Valentine's Day of 2005, and thoughts of his Prostate Cancer diagnosis was always on his mind. It was really starting to take a huge toll on his mental being, which was to be expected. The times we spent together were unforgettable, and we really treasured each of them.

We took a trip to Temecula, California and tried our best to block out the Cancer diagnosis. We spent a night in a luxurious five-star resort, relaxing together and having fun. We also did some sightseeing.

Excusing him, he said, "Babe, I will be right back. I have to go to the restroom."

I expected him to come back in a few minutes, but he hadn't. I looked all around in the casino for him, but he was nowhere in sight. Then all of a sudden, he showed up. "Where were you?" I asked.

He just smiled, with that sneaky, huge grin. We then walked up to our hotel room, and as I opened the door, I was completely surprised. There were several balloons, pretty flowers, and Victoria's Secret lingerie arranged so nicely on the bed. What a romantic devil, I thought. With everything that was going on with him, he was still expressing his love for me. I hated to see him going through this ordeal. It hurt my heart as well as my soul, but I have to think positive for his recovery.

Mister's Birthday

"Oh, Lord, please! I need you to do me a favor. Please cure this cancer from Mister's body." I was on my knees, praying. I couldn't make it without him. I couldn't fathom the thought of losing him. Life just wouldn't be the same for me, thinking back on all the special moments we shared over our eight-year relationship, the fun times and the arguments. They were embedded in my memory. Reflecting back on our very last moment together, I could see the reflection of my pain through his eyes. We we're both hurting so badly.

For his birthday, I wanted to surprise him with a dinner reservation at Black Angus. He was pretending to be in good spirits, but I could tell that he was becoming weaker and weaker. We had a cozy, private, romantic spot at the restaurant. He pulled back my chair like a gentleman does for his lady. As we sat down, I noticed that he lost a little more weight. His complexion became a little darker. I was horrified, but I didn't want to react in a way that would make him feel insecure and uncomfortable, so I smiled at him, thinking of the man I met eight years ago.

The man I went out with on our first date—strong and vibrant. The waiter approached us, and I told him that today was my husband's birthday. As

I said those words, a smile formed on Mister's face. It brought joy to his heart, and I realized that I was still so in love with him.

The waiter smiled, "Okay. So, we have a celebration here."

Mister was my husband, In my eyes and in my heart. He did all the things that a good husband does. He always took good care of me—mentally, physically, sexually, and financially—and I loved him dearly for that. I was in it for richer or for poorer, for better or for worse, in sickness and in health, until death do us part.

The waiter took our order, and Mister immediately ordered a club soda. His stomach was nauseous all day. He had been experiencing more pain. He popped two eight hundred milligrams of Ibuprofen into his mouth, while I was grubbing down on a plate of seafood—my favorite crispy golden deep-fried shrimp. He was slowly losing his appetite, so he ordered French Onion Soup.

Normally, Mister could throw down on some seafood, but this time it was different. We wrapped up our date, and on the drive home, I knew he wasn't feeling well. He was getting weaker, so I didn't want him walking me to my door like he always did after our dates. I tried to gather the words so it wouldn't make him feel intimidated and less of a man.

"Babe, it's too late. I know you have a busy schedule tomorrow. Don't worry about walking me to my door. I'll be alright," I said, but he just insisted.

YETTA YVETTE

"I opened the doors for you in the beginning of our relationship. I'm sick, but that isn't going to stop me now. I'm going to open your doors baby until the end. Until I die!" I smiled, gave him a quick peck on his lips, and said, "Good Night!"

The Promise

It was a dark dreary evening, a little after six thirty. Mister called me, and he wanted to discuss something really important. I could hear the urgency in his voice, and I prepared myself for the uncertainty. What did he want to talk about? He arrived by seven o'clock.

I stepped out of my house, looking like a supermodel as he would often tell me, and we drove to a nearby golf course. We pulled in the parking lot, and he parked his truck.

"What's on your mind, honey?" I said. "I've been thinking about a lot lately," he said. "I don't know what God's plan is for me. Lately, my health is up and down. I don't feel like I used to anymore. This cancer is taking a toll on my body. I have no control over it. I'm popping painkillers, not one but two of them Strong shit like jelly beans. I'm getting weaker and weaker, baby, with each passing day."

My eyes began to tear up. I hated to hear him talking like this. I could see how much anguish he was in. I was so scared.

He continued, "If I die, I want you to know that I love you. I want you to have all of my personal belongings, and also, I have some money put away for you. I have it all set up in my Last Will and Testament for you." Then he added, "I'm not too worried about my family. I gave all of them an amazing lifestyle. My kids, I provided them best education so they would able to take care of themselves. Sharon is good. They can't be upset with my decision and last wishes. And if they ever will be, oh well, I'll be long dead and gone. So, I'm not worried about any of them, only you! Because of you, I was able to go on in my life. You are a huge part of my life. I don't want you suffering or wanting for nothing, baby. You gave me happiness and love. You showed me a different world. I needed the balance that you gave me. I needed a friend, and you became my best friend. We blossomed into something beautiful and only because I was a very unhappy man. I have no regrets about us, and if I were to do it all over again, I wouldn't change a thing. I would still go after you all over again. Don't you feel bad, okay? Promise me something."

I was already bawling at this point. It sounded like he was giving up on his fight.

He said, "Promise me that you will love again and marry. You have to have a baby. Promise me that you'll be the best at whatever you choose to do, career-wise. You have to challenge yourself to be the best that you can be. Promise me that you'll always care about yourself. Please, never let no man treat you less than you deserve. If I die and you let another man treat you unworthy, I will come back and haunt you."

I smiled from his humor.

"I treated you like the queen that you are. Baby,

always keep your health up. Please don't become overweight. Promise that you will start a business. You have to do that. I will be watching and cheering you on. Lastly, promise me that you will not do anything irrational. No suicide! You hear me?"

With tears in my eyes, I responded, "Yes, I promise." He just wanted my happiness and the best for me. I gave him my solemn promises.

The last words he said to me were, "Yetta Yvette, if I die and you never find love like what we have, true love, just know this: You have a man right here"— pointing at his chest— "who loves you to death. I will be loving you from the sky."

～

A few days later, I went away to Las Vegas to see my family. From there, I called Mister, but I didn't get a response. The next day came, and still there was no response. I called and called. It was unlike him to not return my phone calls. I began to worry, and I didn't know what to do until it finally hit me.

I called the hospital where he was given his care before. Sharon answered the telephone. I wanted to hang up in her face, but I had to find out what was going on with my baby. She informed me that Mister had to be rushed to the hospital. It wasn't looking good for him this time. See, Mister kept some important information from me. Prior to this, he had to be rushed to the hospital for the first time for an emergency blood transfusion. He had been complaining to me about his arm. It was sore and in pain and was absolutely bothering him, so I encouraged him to make an appointment to the doctor. The doctors inserted a device for his radiation and chemotherapy treatments, and this device ended up causing an infection. It contaminated his blood and poisoned his entire system and had to have a blood transfusion immediately, or else, he would die instantly.

It all started to make sense to me, the reason why he was always cold and weak. He didn't tell me because he didn't want me to worry. After I got off the telephone, I immediately broke down and cried. I had to get to the hospital. I was shaking and trembling out of control, like a drug addict in need of a fix. I wasn't in any condition to drive, so my mother drove us. She got us to California within four hours, and I rushed straight to the hospital.

I didn't care that the family would be there. The secret would be exposed. Sharon already knew about us. Once we arrived inside, I checked in at the front desk. The nurse looked at a clipboard with paperwork on it and said, "Who are you here to see?" I told her Mister's name, and she walked away to a room adjacent to the front desk. Mister was in that room.

The nurse returned with a bit of bad news for me. "His wife doesn't want you in the room."

The hurt suddenly came over me. A male nurse later came out of the room. He motioned over to me to come to the side of the corridor and told me, "Mister's condition had been downgraded to terminal." When I heard the word "terminal," I went hysterical. I lost all control over of me. The man that I loved with all of my heart, more than anything in the world, was dying in his hospital bed just a few footsteps away. I couldn't even see him for the last time to say good-bye. All I could do was turn to my mother and cry on her shoulder. I left the hospital in despair.

On the ride home, all I could think about was eight years of memories flashing before me. I was losing my superman, my love.

Then my mother said, "It was probably best that you didn't see him like that, lying in the hospital bed helplessly, with tubes running all through his body. I know you would have gone berserk if you had witnessed it."

No, I certainly didn't want to see him like that, so I tried to look at it from her perspective. She was absolutely correct about it. I would have gone berserk. I knew I would have.

Without a Sound

I flashed back into time. It was a nice and peaceful Sunday, and Mister and I were watching the movie Madea. We wanted to escape and have some laughs for a few hours. We arrived at the theater earlier, so we had time to talk before our movie started.

He said to me, "Babe, I have never been so afraid in my entire life, but I'm afraid to die." A tear was streaming down his worried face.

The powerful man, whom I witnessed a lot of times cussing and fussing at his uncooperative customers in the office, was having a moment of despair. Do you know how it is to see a man cry? It leaves you completely, without a sound. At first, I didn't know what to say. Over the years, I had seen him shed a tear or two—the time in San Diego in our hotel room and the time that he cried when I cried. But this time, the situation was much different.

Death was involved here, and we didn't have any idea of what was to come for us. I slowly lifted his head and, looking at him deep in his eyes, said, "I know, babe, but we don't have to be scared. I'm right here by your side. And guess what? I'm not going anywhere."

I suggested that we needed to go to church.

Mister believed in God. He wasn't one to attend church regularly, but he did attend to one. I knew that would make us feel so much better, so we did just that.

Church became our sanctuary. It was where we needed to go and what we needed to do. We prayed together for our sins and cried together as we had no idea what the final outcome of it all was.

I prayed for a miracle from God above. "Dear Lord! If you are listening, please, please ease his pain. Heal his body from this cancer."

My nerves were so rattled that I needed to take a sedative in order to calm myself down. I felt like I was going to have an instant heart attack. My heart was in distress. It felt like it had a huge hole in it. The sedatives eventually started to kick in. They were causing my body to relax. I was drifting into unconsciousness until I was knocked out. I awoke the next morning just hoping that it was all a horrible nightmare, and my cell phone rang then.

It was Sharon, and she said, "He passed onto Heaven." She was calling to inform me of the funeral arrangements. The funeral was going to be held on the upcoming Saturday at ten o'clock.

After I got off of the phone, I fell to the floor, crying. "No! No!" I cried in despair.

From this point on, my life was going to look dim. How was I going to make it without him? It wasn't about the money. Financially, I could take care of myself. It was all about Mister—the love, companionship, laughter, all the fun times we shared. How was I supposed to go on with my life?

I was on my own now.

I awoke Saturday morning wanting to believe that it was just a horrible nightmare. But it was my reality. Mister was dead and gone. I had to somehow mentally prepare myself for his funeral service. How was I going to react viewing his lifeless body lying in a casket, with the thoughts of our very last time together?

If I had known that his birthday would be our last time together, I would have kissed him passionately instead of just the quick peck that I gave him and said all the things that I could and should have said to him. But I didn't. I told him several times previously in our conversations, but I would have reiterated them. Now, it was too late for me to say anything.

There were so many signs— his voice, loss of appetite, darkened complexion, the constant pill-popping, and becoming weaker and weaker—but I chose to ignore it all. I wanted to believe so desperately that he would pull through and beat it. He was my superman.

I started dressing for the funeral. My body feeling numb, and my eyes kept pouring out tears, as well as my soul. At first, I heard a voice telling me, "Yvette, you shouldn't go! Remember him the way you did—strong, aggressive, charismatic, and a caring man." I couldn't do that; I loved him, too much. It would be last time seeing him ever again. It would be a confirmation that he had gone onto heaven. My family attended the funeral service with me. They had to pay their last respects for me too.

Although, they were against our relationship in the very beginning, they now sympathized with me.

Our Last Intimate Moment

Flashing back into time, I should have seen the red flag. Mister was becoming thinner. He was starting to look a little different.

He said to me, "Baby, I don't know why, but my stomach is hurting so badly. I just took two Ibuprofen four hours ago, and it's still bothering me."

I rushed to the kitchen to get him a glass of water so he could take two more pills. The look in his eyes showed a sign of fear I had never seen from him before, as if he knew that the cancer was spreading to the rest of his body.

We started watching television together. I noticed his hair had grown out. Being a licensed cosmetologist, I always stayed prepared with my shears in my purse, so I hooked him up with a nice haircut. As I was cutting his hair, we conversed about the news. We talked about all the crazy events that were occurring in the world at the time. We shared a few laughs. Although, I knew it had to hurt him to laugh, I still tried to be humorous to keep his spirits lifted.

"Babe, are you almost finished? I know you hooked it up." He looked at me and gave me that nice Kool-Aid grin. He had grown weary and couldn't sit any longer. Once I finished cutting his hair, I cleaned up the hair from the floor. Then he walked over to lie down on the bed.

The pain running all through his body, the cancer had taken the man, who was once jolly with a beautiful personality away from me.

I walked to the bed and told him, "Babe, I would like to give you a massage. I think that would make you feel a little better, if that is all right with you?"

He smiled and nodded, "Yes, I would love that."

I massaged his body, trying my best to ease his pain, and occasionally rubbed his head until he fell asleep. Seeing him like this was killing me softly. I got in the bed and cuddled next to him until I fell asleep.

I should have seen all of the signs that his health was deteriorating, because he once told me earlier on in our relationship that the only way that he wouldn't want to touch me anymore was if he got sick. I should have known then that this would be our last intimate moment.

The Funeral

I was nervous as we drove to the church. The time was approaching nearer. I looked to see his family, pulling up, in a long black stretched limousine. Sharon, son, daughter, and various other family members. I couldn't help, but feel cheated. I should have been riding in the limo. In my heart, I was family too, but due to the certain circumstances. I was a secret.

We get out of the car, and walk towards the church. Once we arrived inside, I approached Sharon. She was dressed all in black, from head to toe. We exchanged hellos. I was polite. I gave her a card of bereavement. I felt she should of given me one too, but she didn't.

She had this strange look on her face. She probably wasn't expecting me to show, but I did. I know she was afraid. I'm sure. My family, and I walked inside the church. The church was packed with people. Some people even had to stand up against the walls. One thing for sure. Mister had love in the room that day. He had a strong impact over so many. That day proved it.

We located our seats, and wait for the service to start. The services start I hear the cries all around me. I want to breakdown, burst into tears, but I had to hold it inside. I held my tears. Trying to be strong. The minister approaches the pulpit. Reading from his obituary, all of his accomplishments, and all the good deeds, he did for so many people, over the years. He was such an angel. He was that kind of person, one that became successful to make a difference. Not that person who got an attitude, and made a nickel over car fare, thinking that he was the shit who's better than everybody else. No, not Mister. He gave back and helped those he could.

The time came for anyone who wanted to share their personal testimony on what Mister did for them. One by one, people went up to the pulpit. They talked about good times and reminisced about a great man. I wanted to go up, but I didn't, because the secret would be revealed. I knew I wasn't strong enough to do that. He did so much for me. He gave me confidence and a new outlook in life. He taught me to strive and work hard. These were just among the things I learned from watching him, from listening to his talks, and from his encouragements over the eight years that we were together.

The service started to wrap up, and it was quiet. The pallbearer pulled the casket from the outside to inside as I sat there crying, thinking my baby was inside of that casket. Oh, my gosh! Am I going to be able to do this? Okay, breathe, breathe.

My mother, sister, and father looked at me. "Are you sure you want to do this? You don't have to," my mother said.

"Yes," I said. I can do this. It was our turn to

walk up toward the front to the casket to view Mister one last time. I held on to my sister's hand. As I came closer, I was so overwhelmed that I fainted. Thank God my father was there to catch me, or else, I would have hit the floor. I did get a quick glance at Mister, and he was looking as handsome as ever with a smile on his face and his hair neatly groomed. He was wearing a dark blue suit. He was resting in peace, in paradise. The look on his face said it all.

I was crying hysterically as I was walking with my family away from the church. They had the overpass somewhere in Los Angeles, but I didn't attend it, only because with me fainting like that, I was certain that had raised eyebrows, and now people were going to be curious and ask questions.

Who is Mister?

Mister was born in the sticks of Alabama. He was a country boy who became a man but didn't have country ways. He was one of thirteen brothers and sisters and was raised by his mother and stepfather. Mister was a very independent person. At the age of thirteen, he decided to migrate to California to reside with his brother. He took education very seriously. He studied diligently and graduated from junior high and later from Fremont High. He went on to pursue his studies at Cal State University. He labored hard, putting himself through college and working full-time for an aircraft company. He went to school full-time, taking up twelve units. He was the first to graduate from his family, with a Mechanical Engineering degree.

He always had big dreams. Mister worked several jobs during his lifetime, but he had his own drive to become his own boss. He invested and ventured into different lines of businesses, one of which was a cookie shop. It was very successful and pulled in over five thousand dollars monthly. He was in that business for a few years before he went on and developed a trucking company. He won a lot of huge accounts, and this was where he would make his millions.

He was educated, strong, witty, and never self-centered. He always wanted to do what he could to help others—providing employment, motivating people to be at their best, and making cash donations to his favorite charities. This was his personality. When he was in the office, his demeanor was tough, but the businessman behind the desk, the one that I had the opportunity to work for and get to know as a person, was so sweet. He had a huge heart.

He operated the trucking business for more than twenty-five years. He provided employment to several people. Mister, of course, had several obstacles in his life, but his determination and hard work had made him a very successful black entrepreneur. Mister was a high roller, with five different real estate properties. He had two located in California, one in Las Vegas, one in Arizona, and one in Alabama. During his lifetime, he owned ten or more vehicles. With his nonchalant attitude, you would have never known it. He was never boastful, just humble. By watching him, I learned how to be humble too. He once quoted, "If you are blessed with success, that it was a gift, through God. It also takes a lot of hard work, and dedication. God puts certain people, in situations. The reason, and purpose of his "Success," was to help others, and so he did.

Life After Mister

When it was time for the family gathering, the memorial, I couldn't attend it. With me fainting, some may have already wondered and assumed. Mister's body was cremated to ashes, and I couldn't even go to visit him at a grave site. It probably was the best thing for me. It would have been a total remembrance of the reality that he was gone and out of my life.

Instead of going to the gathering, my family and I went to our favorite Mexican food restaurant, El Toritos. The restaurant was one of his favorites too. It was also where we had spent our happy hours after work. He loved their enchiladas and tacos. His favorite for dessert was the Volcano Chocolate Cake with some vanilla ice cream. He would always ask the waiter to microwave it because he liked it warm.

I started to see mirages of him. I cried until my eyes hurt, and my heart ached with agony, as if a dagger was pierced through it. I tried to get myself together. I was up against a fight. I had to go through a healing process, and I had to grieve.

Days went by, I had to come to a realization. I wouldn't receive that daily phone call, anymore. I wouldn't hear his voice, anymore. I had that burning sensation in my heart, that feeling you get when you miss a person so badly. He wasn't ever coming back to me, and it was hard for me to contemplate.

I stared at my cell phone in disbelief, wanting my cell phone to ring again and to be able to talk to him. I just couldn't believe it. He was gone, and he was never coming back! Everywhere I went in California was a total remembrance of all the things and places we used to do and go to, like the clubs, restaurants, amusement parks, movie theaters, the beaches, and the shopping malls. I would often flashback into that time.

In my mind, I needed to escape from it all.

The man came into my life when I was twenty-four years old, and at the age of thirty-three, I experienced the ultimate loss of love. Mister passed on earlier in the summer. My birthday was fast approaching in August. It was going to be my very first birthday without him. I kept thinking about the past, all the laughter, fun times, arguments, jealousy, insecurities, and the lovemaking. I was in a horrible state of mind.

My family tried their best to keep me occupied by trying to get me out of the house, but I wasn't in the mood to do anything or to be around anyone. It was as if my brain was dead and my heart flatlined. I felt dead, like a zombie. My soul had left my body, but I was walking around in existence. Every day was very difficult to cope with. I slept and slept for hours, dreaming of him and his golden smile shining so brightly that it would light up a room. Food didn't taste the same for me anymore. I lost my appetite, and I didn't care anymore.

On many occasions, I thought that I was going to have a nervous breakdown. Instead, I went into a very deep depression. I constantly awoke to crying, and all I could do was reflect on thoughts of my past with Mister. I was blessed with eight wonderful years of memories with him. His voice, I missed so much. I had a previous tape recording of his voice, and I listened to that over again. I wanted to talk to him so badly that I cried uncontrollably. I wanted to talk to him one last time so I could tell him all the things that I didn't get the chance to say. I wanted to let him know again how much I loved him. For anyone who has lost their other half, you can sympathize with me.

When you are happy, and you put in some years with a person, and your everyday life consist of them. Then suddenly, you are without them, you're feeling lost. I was so lost, searching for a way in my heart to try to be strong. It hurt so bad. Losing a family member is totally different from losing your other half, although any loss of a loved one is hard to cope with. But this was even tougher, so in order to help me cope with the absence of Mister, I wrote it in a journal. Whenever I wanted to talk to him, I wrote in my black journal.

If I had some good news, or if I wanted to inform him on how my day was going, I wrote all the time. I know it probably may sound silly to you, but this was what I did. I know I should have seen a grief counselor or a therapist or something. But I didn't. Writing was my way of dealing and coping with my pain.

During this time, I did what I needed to do. It was my time to grieve, and that was exactly what I did. I focused on me and didn't try to jump quickly into another relationship, for it wasn't the solution for me. I gave myself plenty of time to grieve. When the holidays came around, I felt it the most. I was so lonely inside I had to learn how to be alone. My new reality soon set in. I had to try to continue on with my life. I had to take care of myself, but how? I wasn't a stranger to hard work. I knew how to work, but after Mister's death, I would never be that same person as before.

There were moments when I became despondent, and I would just blank out from time to time. I could only reflect back on one of our last conversations, the one we had in the truck when we were at the golf course. It kept flashing in my mind. He told me that he took care of everything, and obviously, I trusted him. I had enough money to only carry me for about a year, and then after that the bill collectors would start calling. The life I had before with Mister was so different from the one that I have now. To start, I had to learn how to budget.

In the beginning, I didn't know what it meant to budget. If I saw an outfit or something I liked, I just purchased it. It didn't matter what the price was. I spent money like it was water. It was always running through my hands that I couldn't hold on to it. I was crazy back then, and things were different now. I prayed, "Oh, God, help me! How do I go back to a regular lifestyle?" It was now all like a good dream.

I had been exposed to a lifestyle of luxury, with no worries or wants for nothing. I had a man who had my back and supported me in every decision in my life, and now I was alone.

Then my cell phone rang. It was a call from an unexpected and unknown area code. At first, I wasn't going to answer it, but then I listened to my inner intuition. "Hello," I said.

"Hello, Yvette! It's Sharon!" I was absolutely shocked to be hearing from her. She asked, "How are you doing?"

I was just trying to hang in there. It was all that I could do. I replied, "I'm hanging in here, you know?"

During our conversation, she expressed that she knew that Mister really cared for me. He showed it in his eyes every time she would mention my name. I listened, waiting for her to discuss Mister's will, but she never mentioned it. Instead, she asked, "Do you want me to return this nutritional book back to you?" It was a book with healthy remedies for illnesses.

My father loaned it to Mister while he was having his cancer treatments. "Yes!" I said, so I gave her my address. After I got off the telephone, I started to contemplate about our conversation.

Something was really fishy about it all. Why would she care about returning a book to me? I assumed that she was using the book as an excuse to get my address, so she could mail the documents for Mister's Last Will and Testament. I confirmed the address so she could mail it out. Mister did make it clear to me, in our very last conversation that his attorney would call me. Days after, I rushed to the mailbox, but it was always empty.

A week passed on, but there was no book or letter. Another week passed, and still nothing, so I called the upstairs phone number. The phone just rang, but after three rings, I got a recording saying that the phone number had been disconnected. Next, I called the downstairs phone number. I got the same recording again. Both phone numbers were no longer in service, disconnected. What's going on here? I thought. It wasn't adding up.

There was no way for me to get in contact with her. How can I get in contact with her now? I had to be an investigator. I located a service that assists you with locating people. Once I put in her name and information, all of her new contact information came up on my computer screen. She moved to the valley, and she had a new phone number. Thank God for computers!

So, I called her and she answered the telephone. "Hello?" I said, a little nervous inside. She recognized my voice. You could hear in her voice that she was really shocked to be hearing from me.

"How are you?" I asked her. "Did you ever get a chance to mail out that nutritional book?" I expressed the importance that it meant to my father.

"I thought you didn't want it back."

"What? I never said that." Where in the hell did she get that from? It was my father's book. It wasn't my property. She irritated me to the extreme. It didn't make any sense to me. What was her initial reason for calling me if she wasn't planning on mailing out the book to me? And that was when it hit me. Maybe that was her way of trying to find out if I knew I was in Mister's will. He mentioned it to me right before he died, so, I gathered up the nerves to ask her about it. This was when all hell broke loose.

She went off on me and started using all kinds of profanity. "How in the fuck did you have the nerve to ask me about that? I know you guys were together. You are not going to be happy. Since you destroyed my life, yours will be destroyed, with no husband or a family. Nobody's going to want your ass."

But what struck me the most was when she said to me, "Mister didn't work for you. He worked for me and my damn family. Whatever shit you got out of him during your relationship, that is all you're going to get."

She went on, "How dare you carry on the way you did, causing all that fucking drama at the funeral! Your boyfriend is dead now!"

Of course, she was upset about it, but what happened at the funeral wasn't an act for me. It was my love for Mister. I wanted to crawl up in the casket that day. I felt dead. Little did she know, but he was my fiancé. The conversation went pretty bad. Plenty of words of anger were tossed between us, back and forth.

How could she be so cruel to me? It wasn't my fault the relationship started. I couldn't believe it.

Why was she getting all upset now and trying to hurt me with her words, like it was all a surprise to her. I knew it had to hurt, but it wasn't my fault. I knew there had to be more to it than just that nutritional book. I knew it. After we argued for about ten minutes, I ended the conversation with what would hurt her the most.

She hurt me, so I had to retaliate. "Okay, you may have all the money, but I have something that is way more important than anything, and you can't take it away from me. I had a man who loved me with all of his heart. The memories, all the mentoring, and knowledge, you could never ever take them away. To me, that was worth more than money because I know with hard work, I can always get the money back." When I said that, she hung up the phone.

I grew frustrated, knowing what had happened. It was time for me to take action. I called up an attorney for advice. I was up for a fight. I didn't have much money now, and the cost for attorneys and courts could be very expensive. Plus, she had a son-in-law who had his own law firm. It was going to be tough, but I proceeded to hire an attorney, anyway.

The attorney explained to me the
situation. He said, "It was going to be a difficult one because I didn't have legal documentation."

I needed paperwork stating what belongings Mister wanted me to have. Since Sharon was still legally married to him, she was the executor of his estate. I didn't think to get it all in writing. How could I? I was distraught at that time. I was losing a man that I loved with all my heart. The attorney suggested that we try a bluff tactic, and I tried it in hopes that it would work, but it didn't.

She was ready to go to court too. All I had were photographs of us together for eight years, a promise with an engagement ring, and appraisal paperwork. I didn't have the actual paperwork that stated what belongings he wanted me to have. Besides, I didn't have money for court cost. I was in a hell of a crazy situation. I had to make up in my mind that I would have to start all over. I had to go looking for a job in order to get the money to start up my business. It became overwhelming.

For eight years of my life, I was with a multimillionaire who gave me everything. Now, I had to go out looking for a job. Some days, it was difficult to be positive. I had days when I wanted to give up and just throw in the towel, but I kept hearing Mister's voice in that last conversation we had where he said, "I will be your guardian angel. I will be watching over you. If I know that you are struggling ever in the world, I'm not resting because that was not my purpose with you. I wanted you to have the best in life, with no worries or struggles."

I cried to the point where I started to get a damn headache. I reminisced about how things used to be. I had a new reality to face, and it was looking dim. It took everything in me just to keep going on. It was difficult to roll out of the bed in the morning. Once again, I heard his voice. "C'mon, get out of that bed, girl. You'll have plenty of time to rest when you are dead and gone."

He would always say this to me, one of the many reasons that always kept me so motivated. The lacerations of my heart, and soul were draining my body. I was feeling so weak and lost, as if someone had exhausted all the blood out of my body. I had these terrible thoughts of suicide. The demons kept on at my mind and seemed to be picking and pulling at my soul. It kept saying, "C'mon, do it! Do it!"

Satan was working hard on me. I contemplated taking a bottle of sleeping pills and just getting it all over with. But Mister's promises kept going over and over in my head.

He was saying, "Get your head right, girl! You are tougher than that.

Then, I heard God saying, "You are tougher than that. I created you."

Mister's voice again, "Don't disappoint me, remember what you promised? Don't take the simple way out. You promised me that you wouldn't do that. I love you."

I remembered the look in his eyes when I made the promises to him.

I kept flashing back to the time in the car at the golf course. Me taking the easy way out would only disappoint him, not to mention my family. I just couldn't do it. It hurt my heart. I had to be strong for all of them. My faith became stronger, but questioning God was what I did on a regular basis. How could God call such a wonderful man home to

Heaven when there was still so much good for him to do in this world? Like they say, the good always die young.

At first, I couldn't comprehend it, but as time progressed, I started to realize that Mister came into my life for a reason. It was all for a purpose, and that purpose was to enlighten me about life. He was there to show me a better lifestyle so I could aim highly and have higher expectation out of life. He was there to mentor me and guide me with my business. It became transparent to me. If I could turn back the hands of time, would I want to do things differently?

My answer would be absolutely no. Besides, it shaped me into the woman I am today. My only regret would be that I didn't get everything in writing. I was in need of prayer, so I turned to a preacher, who took me in for some prayer time. I prayed more and more for strength and forgiveness of my sin so I could carry on in this life. After a few months of grieving, I was finally adjusting and settling into my new atmosphere pretty well.

One day, we were having our television cable installed. The technician rang the doorbell three times. He was a nice-looking black cable guy and also very well-mannered. He asked my mother several questions, like where we came from before we moved to Vegas, if we liked it here. He kept staring at me. He was flirting and seemed to be interested in me.

I pretended that I couldn't see it, so I ignored him. It had only been about two and a half months since Mister's death. I was so out of touch with life. My mind was floating in the clouds. My mother, of course, had to play the matchmaker, and I hated it when she did that. I gave her a look that meant "Stop!"

"What's wrong with her?" he asked. "She seems so sad and despondent."

"Oh, she just lost her fiancé to death," my mother said. My family felt that the best remedy for me was to get involved in another relationship quickly. Maybe it would have been for most people, but I just couldn't do it. It was so weird. I had the feeling that I would be cheating on Mister if I did; therefore, I didn't want to. Even though Mister wasn't here on this earth anymore, I just couldn't let someone else get close to me or touch me. It would feel so weird.

Jamel, the cable guy insisted that he only wanted to be my friend. He had just broken up with his girlfriend. He said, "I need a friend too," so I gave him my telephone number.

We began to have only phone conversations—just as friends. He was a great guy, but there was no love connection or chemistry between us. My heart was still overflowing with so much love for Mister. It was time to gradually get myself back into life. I had been off from work for about a whole year. It was time to focus on making money again. I needed to get my career going.

Early mornings I was up, and I went looking for a job. I started working for a car repossession company. I worked there for about three months, and then I quit. Actually, they let me go, and the decision was mutual. I was brought in the office on a Friday afternoon, but before they could even get the words out, I told them I would resign. I wasn't into the job. I already had a heavy load on my mindset with the loss of Mister, so I needed an easier job. I didn't need anything too brain-boggling or stressful. I had to gradually work myself back into the workforce.

Next on the list was a sales position for a contract company. I did that for six weeks and then quit, only because another position that I really wanted became available. The position was for a clerk typist at a timeshare resort. I could be comfortable with this. It was what I was familiar with. I dressed sharp in my black business suit, looking all fresh, and went in for an interview. I said all the right words that would land me the position. I was given the position right on the spot.

I started my new job right around the time of the NBA All-Star weekend in 2007. I was so excited. It would be a place to go and a reason for me to want to get my day started. This time around, I would be working with a room full of females. It was about four women, to be exact. I work better with men, only because women can sometimes cause so much drama. I didn't want to be a part of any of that. I went to work every day and stayed away from the gossiping. I checked in with my supervisor. There was so much gossip always going on, but I kept to myself. When I went to work, I made sure that I followed Mister's advice about dressing and looking good. When I stepped out of my house, I was looking like a supermodel. Of course, this would start a lot of hateration. I didn't care. It was just me. Six months passed and things were all right with my new job.

One day, Anthony a new supervisor, who moved from the Orlando Resort, came in. He made a transfer to come and work with us on the West Coast. He was an eye candy, light-skinned, had pretty smile, and with muscular physique. I noticed him, but I wasn't head over heels, like most of the ladies in the office. I was still grieving for Mister. I was taking it one day at a time.

For me, I felt that I wasn't ready for a relationship. He flirted with me, playing those kiddy games like tapping me on my shoulder from behind. You know how guys in school did it when they had a schoolboy crush on you. He was giving me compliments on a daily basis with a flirty look in his eyes. I was always leery about getting involved with people I worked with. It was unethical.

I heard a voice again, Mister's voice. He was telling me, "It's all right." If I was interested in him, I had his approval. I was ecstatic, and I went to work more excited. I had never felt happier about work before. I was trying to impress him in every way, with my attitude and my look. I envisioned a kiss with him. It had been three years since I had been with anyone. It was so difficult to fathom, kissing and making love to someone else other than Mister.

On this day, I had to get away from the

monotony of work for a minute. While walking to the restroom, Anthony came walking out of the men's restroom. All of a sudden, we had a moment. I could hear the music. He looked deeply into my eyes, as I did the same. He came closer to me, pulling me toward him. I felt so awkward. We were kissing in the hallway. Afterward, he went his way, and I went on mine. I continued on to the ladies' restroom. I couldn't believe it. I felt the butterflies in my stomach, and my heart was pounding faster and faster.

From that moment on, things would never be the same again, for us. I felt the chemistry between us, but working relationships are so difficult to maintain. To tell you the truth, I am totally against relationships at work, because if it doesn't work out, then you have to face the person every day at work, making it very uncomfortable to make your paper.

So instead, we decided to remain only as friends. I invited him over for Thanksgiving dinner. We hung out, and it was fun spending time with him and having the idea of someone else new in my life.

My Guardian Angel

No matter where I was or what I was doing, I would always hear the "voice." It was not that I was going crazy, although a situation like I experienced could have easily made me so, but sometimes I could really hear it. A voice directed me in certain situations, or it facilitated certain business decisions for me. It even protected me.

While driving to work, I was running fifteen minutes behind schedule. My work shift began at nine thirty in the morning. It was nine forty-five when the unthinkable occurred, and it stood out in my memory, because it was one of those life-or-death moments of my life. I was driving closer to an erratic driver who was trying to speed up to beat the oncoming traffic. He raced out of the parking lot, but instead of waiting until the traffic would die down, he erratically lost control of his vehicle and slammed into a traffic pole.

The voice then came to me and it said, "Drive fast, faster, Hurry! Hurry! Move!" As I approached the traffic pole, I drove my jeep quickly, making a quick lane change. Seconds later, I turned to look behind me, and all I could witness was this tower of a traffic pole crashing down. My heart beat like the sounds of a drum. It felt like the movie Final Destination, so I was pretty shaken afterward. Once

I arrived at work, I explained the reason for my tardiness. Of course, my supervisor and coworkers were all happy that everything was all right with me. I was on edge all day, because I kept thinking it could have been the end for me.

My guardian angel was looking over me. I could feel the power of the shield that protected me. His voice, I know it was him. He told me that he would be watching over me. My guardian angel.

Life's Uncertainties

Can you imagine winning a million-dollar lottery only to lose it all after a few years? Everything was so very different, and now I was having to get used to the alteration of a whole new lifestyle. Before, I was loving all the finer material things that life had to offer. At the age of twenty-five, I was rolling around in a Rolls Royce and Mercedes Benz, given expensive gifts, and never had to worry about bills, so, I was accustomed to an unbelievable lifestyle. This was how it was for me.

Now, knowing that I was going to have to start fresh all over again, it wouldn't be so easy for me. Because of my badly damaged heart. Which means I had to put in some hard work, and find me. The economy took a turn for the worst. People weren't vacationing like they used to and our vacationing sales plummeted. We had a huge meeting, discussing the challenges and changes that were going to occur within the company.

After the holidays, my entire department received our pink slips while I was on a medical leave due to a car accident that I had gotten into after the company Christmas party.

Around one o'clock, late on Friday night, I was struck from behind by some teenage kids. While driving home, I was sitting at a red light when I heard the screeching sounds of tires. I looked in the rear-view mirror and saw a truck slamming me smack in the back of my jeep. I cried hysterically, because I envisioned my car being totaled.

Once I got out of the car, there were only minor damages and they had insurance, so it was covered. But due to the sudden impact, it caused me to need physical therapy. I slightly became dependent on painkillers to deal with my back pain.

~

Some days were good, and others just weren't. This wasn't a good one.

It was January 2009. One day, I received a telephone call from Gina, informing me that we had all been laid-off. I worked for this company for two years, and just like that I was unemployed. I was unemployed, and all dignity within myself was stripped away from me. The world chewed me up and then spit me out. Because of the recession, it was now going to be very difficult for me—a highly skilled, smart, and intelligent woman—to locate a job. I felt like I was on a checker board, unable to make a move. I was stuck in one spot, a black square. It was dark, and I was going around, spinning in circles.

Then I came up with the notion to invest all my energies of searching for a job, and I put it all in me. Overall, that was the original plan, in the first place. Part of me, still dealing with the pain of grieving, and the unknowing of my future.

Psychologically, my state of mind wasn't capable of operating or making good and sound decisions, so how could I run a business? Of course, I did have my fears too. Am I ready? I questioned myself. I was going all in.

Life could be like a roller coaster. One minute, you are up, and the next, you are crashing down. I tried to be optimistic about it all, believing that sometimes things happen in life to make you come to a realization. It was time for me to get things in order for business, my very own business. I did have the thoughts of failure in my head. Could I do it without Mister here now? He was my mentor, and a great teacher, so now it was time for me to show that I could be an excellent student. The developments of Anytyme Baskets were on their way.

I worked day and night relentlessly, composing a website and getting marketing together. The worries of going to work were no longer on my mind. God has a way of working miracles. For most, being laid-off was a tragedy, but for me, it was a blessing. I worked, worked, and worked. I didn't have a boyfriend. I kept busy and focused. I wanted to be in control of my own destiny. I was moving forward. I was on the right track to a whole new life when my health issue started to take its toll on me again.

I stressed so much in the years of Mister's death that my only fibroid came back. The doctor was unable to remove one because it was a huge health risk. It grew bigger, but this time, it was no longer the size of a grapefruit. The doctors did warn me. It was possible that it could come back at any time, depending on my diet, stress, and hormone levels, and it did with a vengeance. It gave me pain that was indescribable, all the symptoms as before, only worse. I knew it was because of the trauma of losing Mister.

I couldn't eat, and I didn't have an appetite. When I was able to eat, my diet altered. I wasn't eating healthy at first-class restaurants like I used to do with Mister before. I became a connoisseur of junk food. I had to meet with Mister Joseph, a nutritionist from Santa Monica, California. He explained to me what I needed to do in order to become healthy and get rid of the fibroid. It was challenging. I had to go through this crazy detoxification diet. My new diet consisted of no fried foods, salad dressing for taste, sugar and dairy; just veggies. Basically, I wasn't able to eat too much. I dropped from size 7/8 to 5/6, and I was feeling awesome, with more confidence.

From time to time, I kept in touch with Anthony from the resort. He was like all the rest of us and trying to get back into the grind of the workforce. He was having problems with finding another job. Eventually, it caused him to have to relocate back to Orlando, Florida. At first, I thought that my heart wasn't capable of loving again, but with him, I knew it could happen. It just didn't work out between us. We were too much alike.

One major thing that we had in common is that we shared the same birthday. Can you believe that?

The expectation of how we wanted our life to be, sometimes it just never happens like the way you want it. For me, I didn't anticipate my life to turn out this way. At this point in my life, I wasn't planning it anymore. We live in an era of the unexpected, life's uncertainties. Don't misinterpret me when I say not to plan life. By all means, I'm not advocating that you not plan your career, travels, or when to have your children. I'm just saying that when it comes to "love." Now that is a topic, we really have no control over, because we never know who we're going to fall in love with and who is going to be digging us. Pressing forward, my motto is "living and taking it one day at a time."

Learning How to Love Again

The thought of dating again made me bug out. I had to learn to love another man over again, and a part of me rebelled in the beginning. I wanted to be in another meaningful relationship, and at the same time, I was afraid to. I was afraid of going through the dating process. When you lose your other half to death, your heart is damaged. For me, it was difficult getting close to someone. I was scared to get close. I had major trust issues, so I buried myself into my work so I wouldn't concentrate on a relationship. I assured myself, when God has the right man for me, it will happen.

Hopefully that man would be able to understand everything that I had gone through. He would need to be able to be patient with me and love me in a way that is unconditional. After all that occurred in the past, I was beginning to feel guilty again for what I had done. I flashed back to hearing my argument with Sharon. I thought about the conversation in depth. I kept hearing the part when she said that I wasn't going to be happy, with no husband or a family. It worked on my mental state. I started to feel like that was why a good man wasn't showing up in my life.

On top of it all, because of Mister, the next man to come into my life would have to deal with the ultimate amount of pressure from me. I didn't like to compare the past with the present, but it was sure to happen in this case. I became very selective when it came to dating men. I couldn't just get on with any old man. He had to be strong, a go-getter with a positive mindset, a divine winner. So, until the time this man would present himself to me, I worked and worked.

It was all I could do at the time until the month of March, ninth day came along. The day was dark and gloomy, exactly the way I was feeling inside. I had to run some errands, and first stop was the bank. Instead of going to my normal branch and handling my business, the voice came to me again. "No! No! Go to the other bank branch!" The drive was about fifteen minutes away from my usual bank branch, but I said, what the hell?

I arrived at the bank and walked up to the line. I was patiently waiting behind a guy. After he finished his transaction, he said, "The ATM machine is all yours." He smiled, and I smiled back.

When I approached the ATM machine, I couldn't help but notice that he had stepped outside. It looked like he was waiting for me, so I finished up with my transaction and stepped outside. He was on his cell phone, wrapping up a business call. He was handsome, with almond brown skin, his height about five feet and ten inches. He was wearing athlete gear, and he looked like he could be a ball player. I started to walk toward my car.

When suddenly, he approached me. Is this man

really stepping to me? He is walking closer, and closer. "Excuse me, Miss!" Can I talk to you for a minute?" Hisapproach was very gentleman-like, and he got big points with me for that.

With his respectable approach, I knew he wasn't from this town, so I was checking this guy out. Before I could give him my seven digits, disguising my look and playing it Crazy Sexy Cool, I was checking him out from head down to his Nikes.

"My name is Devon." I just relocated here from New York City," he said.

I knew it! Was he the player kind? I didn't know, but I would take a gamble and find out. We exchanged business cards. Okay, his profession was in real estate. We talked for ten minutes and then went our separate ways.

He called me the next day. I am totally old school, and I believe that a man should always make the first approach, at least, in the very beginning of dating.

What can I say? I'm a lady, and I was raised that way. It was a Saturday night, and my cell phone rang. I was so nervous inside.

"Hello!" My tone sounding excited.

"How are you?" he responded, and we had a great conversation for about thirty minutes.

We made the arrangements for our very first date the following day, on a Sunday at eight o'clock in the evening. After I hung up the telephone, I felt a rush of excitement come over me. I had been out of the game for about seven years. I was like a benchwarmer, waiting to go into the basketball game. The alarm sounded, and it was time for me to play.

It was date night.

The only thing that I disliked about dating was the uncertainty, never knowing what kind of person you are getting involved with. The process of having to detect the lies from the truth. Especially when you fall, in the older age category. I didn't want to have to deal with married guys anymore, with baby mama drama, or with finding out that he's bisexual.

I said a prayer while driving to our meeting location, which was at Town Square Mall. I had never been there before. Please, Lord, I pray that this guy is worth my time. I parked my ride and waited in front of the food store for him to arrive. I was a few minutes early. The anxiety was overwhelming. Did I check him out correctly the first time we met? I hoped he looked the same—handsome. I patiently waited. About 7:55 p.m., a light tan sophisticated caddy pulled up. I thought, nice!

He recognized me. My cell phone rang. "Is that you sitting in front of the whole food store looking beautiful?"

"Thank you! Yes, it's me," I responded.

After he parked his ride, he walked toward me. He was dressed in a cream color suit, looking all fly. He did pass the ride and the dress code inspection test. Now let's see, if this guy can retain my attention. We had dinner at a nice restaurant. While waiting for our meal, the conversation was good.

We discussed our past, of course, our exes had to be a part of it. I couldn't tell much of mine. I gave insights only on what I wanted him to know. I kept from disclosing too much information and mostly kept the topics focused on me.

It was only the first date, and I knew he had his reservations too. He was comedic, with a nice personality. He was recently divorced but without any children. I couldn't believe it. "Are you sure you don't have any kids stashed away somewhere?" I kept asking.

"I wouldn't lie to you about that. Why is

that so hard for you to believe? You're a woman without any children," he said. "By the way, a very nice-looking woman too."

For me, it just seemed so unnatural for a man of his age to not have any children. But he was absolutely correct about me too, so it could be possible for a man, and I trusted him. As I sat there, thinking, I couldn't believe I was out on a date with someone new. Our date was going really well. I enjoyed his company, so now the date was slowly wrapping up.

He walked me to my car, with expectations of a hug and a kiss. Once again, my old fashioned-tradition wouldn't allow it. I said to him, "I don't kiss on the first date."

"Don't be afraid of me." And held out his arms.

Hesitantly, I only gave him a big hug and again said, "Don't be mad at me. I just don't kiss on the first day!" He smiled, and I smiled too.

The night ended on a good note. From this

point on, we had a few late-night phone conversations until our next date. We were becoming more familiar with each other.

On our second date, we met at a nearby casino. I showed up on time, while he was running a few minutes behind. I waited impatiently.

At first, I thought he wasn't going to show up, and then all of sudden, I could see him walking in confidently. I was aggravated a little, but hopefully he had a good reason for being late. We started out the evening with dinner. We ate dinner in the casino, and the setting was romantic, with an animal jungle background. It was very dark and cozy. The date was going very smoothly. We had great conversation, and he was a good company to be around with. I felt secure with him. Plus, he was very funny.

After our dinner, he surprised me with a box of Juicy Couture fragrance. Nice! I liked it when guys go all-out to impress you on the second date. To me, it was really important, especially since I was impressed to the fullest previously.

Our next move was a walk down the Las Vegas Strip. We were walking, holding hands, and sightseeing on the strip. The weather was calm and peaceful. The night was gorgeous, and I was starting anew. Life was feeling meaningful again. Then disaster hit us. Once the date concluded, he walked me to my car. He parked in valet, so I drove him back to his car.

He started patting on his pants pockets only to find out that his wallet was missing. "I can't find my wallet!" He was looking all over in my car—on the floor and on the seats. He checked himself again, and still no wallet anywhere. He realized that somewhere along our date, he lost it.

"Where could it be? We ate at the restaurant. We made a few stops on the strip. My wallet could be anywhere."

I shrugged my shoulders with uncertainty. "I don't know." But he was right. His wallet could have been in three different places that night.

He got out of the car, looking frantically. I was uncertain on what to do next. Do I stay, or do I drive off? The lines in valet were outrageous that night. Friday night was always crazy up there. The cars were quickly racing in and out.

The valet attendant pointed and screamed out to me. "You, keep it moving!"

I told Devon I had to leave, and asked, "So what do you want me to do?" but he didn't hear me because he was all frantic.

As I was leaving, I tried calling him on his cell phone so I could get further instructions on what he wanted me to do, but the call went straight to his voicemail. I panicked, so I drove home. I didn't know what to do.

Our date ended on a sour note. Halfway home, I tried calling him again. I felt so bad for him. Once again, it went straight to his voicemail. I pulled up on my driveway and into my garage, and my dog, Stumpy broke out and escaped from his leash, and I thought, more disaster to come. I ran down the street, trying to get him back before he got hit by a car. While doing so, my cell phone rang. It was Devon. I picked up.

"Hello! Did you find your wallet?" I asked him.

"Yes, I did," he said, but suddenly he was so pissed off with me.

"How could you leave me like that?"

"What?" I tried to explain to him. "I didn't know what to do. I called you twice. It went straight to your voicemail. What was I to do?"

"You were supposed to come back." He gave me the third degree about it, making me feel like a piece of crap.

We argued, and while I was arguing with him, I was still looking for my dog, so I told him, "Can I call you right back? Because Stumpy escaped, and I don't want him to get hit by a car." He became very upset with me.

He replied, "Wow, your dog is more important than me!" Then he suddenly hung up.

I began to worry about Stumpy. Where could he be? Then he suddenly appeared, out of nowhere. After hanging up with him, I started to contemplate about the situation. Was I wrong in this? I felt terrible about it. Sleep didn't come easy that night. I kept thinking about our last conversation. During the conversation, he accused me of being inconsiderate of his feelings. That was not my character. I'm a person who cares. I'm a generous person. How could he be so judgmental of me based on just one time of a catastrophe?

It was way too soon for this to be happening in our relationship, for us. It was only our second date. Could we go forward from this? Would things be different now? He didn't call me, and I didn't call him either. Compatibility was important to me. He was an Aquarius, and me a Leo, and according to our zodiac signs we were supposed to be a great fit for each other. So what is the problem?

Relationships can be a lot of work, especially for me not having been in one for seven years. It was all a learning process over again. What to do? What to say? What not to do? What not to say? Can I trust him? Most of all, I was going to have a huge problem with intimacy. We hadn't spoken all day. I stayed strong and waited for him to call me. He had to make the first move. Finally on a Saturday evening, he called me.

He apologized, and I apologized to him too. The war was over, and we reconciled our differences. We arranged for another date. Tyler Perry's Good Deed had just hit the box office, and I had to see it, and so we agreed to meet there for the movie.

It was Sunday, and I was going to meet with him at two o'clock in the afternoon. I arrived about one forty-five, and our movie started at two thirty. I waited patiently. Then he came walking in so cool and looking handsome as ever. I greeted him with a hug and smile, and we proceeded to walk to the theater.

"Would you like some refreshments?" he asked.

I said no thank you, and we located our seats and waited for the movie to start. Once the movie started, he started talking too, and I was hoping he was not the kind of person who talks all throughout the movie. For sure, he was. I had to shush him up a few times, especially when the couple next to us moved to the rows below just to avoid us. I was totally embarrassed by his constant talking, so I asked him, "Can you go get us some popcorn?"

He said, "I thought you didn't want anything."

I replied, "At that time, I didn't want any refreshments, but I do now."

It was only a test so I could see how he would react to my last-minute decision change. I wanted to know what kind of man he was. Would he blow up on me, or was he patient? He passed the test with flying colors. He returned with a large popcorn and candy, and I was all smiles. The movie was about to begin. The theme focuses on business. I could relate to it. For one, the story was almost somewhat like Mister and me. Secondly, business was my career path, so I paid close attention to it while occasionally, he would say a word or two.

During the movie, his hand grabbed mine, and I looked deep into his bedroom eyes. Then I focused back into the movie. He suddenly turned my head and planted a sensual juicy kiss on my lips. His lips were so soft, and we kissed passionately. My heart was racing and palpitating. The movie concluded with a happy ending, and our next move was to his place.

He wanted to impress me with how he was living. It must have been the bomb. He was so excited to show it off. I am a lady with standards and respect for myself, and I know he couldn't expect sex from me after three dates. Clearly, that was not going to happen. We were driving to his place. He was in his car, and I was in mine, and we got to his location. The neighborhood was so peaceful. He lived in a very nice apartment. Once we parked our cars, walked upstairs, and got inside,

I was astonished. I took a quick tour of his home. I was impressed with how clean his apartment was, knowing that he was a bachelor. We sat on his brown comfy sofa and began to talk more about us. He came closer to me and looked deeply into my eyes, with sparks of passion flying in the air. It was strongly coming over me again.

We passionately kissed, but before I got too overwhelmed with the feelings, I told him, "I need to go."

"C'mon, baby, why?" he said.

"Because I have standards." Plus, I wanted to just take it slowly and for us to really get acquainted with each other more. Also, I was trying to accept the facts that I was kissing, touching, and would be making love to a new man. It had to register not just in my heart but as well as in my brain. He took it all into consideration and wasn't upset about it. Even more, he would respect me. For sure, he knew I wasn't that kind of woman.

Shortly after leaving his apartment, on the drive home, I was happy to be in this place—life and its uncertainties. I didn't know love would find me again. Of course, I prayed for love night and day. I was very particular about my men. I have always been. It took a certain kind of man to be able to deal with a woman like me. I expect the best that a man has to offer to me, or I don't want nothing at all, because I am going to give him my best, a hundred and fifty percent guaranteed.

As a young girl, I was taught to respect myself. I have to love me first, so I think very highly of myself. I am strong like a piece of tough leather, and sometimes it can be very intimidating to a man, especially if he's not strong enough. Most women want a man who is not only strong and can handle his business but also not too He-Man enough to show their sensitive side, to express how much he loves and respects his woman.

I can't take all the credit for my toughness. I owe it to every positive man who had a strong impact in my life, starting with my father who supported his family by working two jobs most of his life in order to provide for us. By having my father present in my life, it gave me stability and guidance, and he kept me level-headed and on the right track.

My Pops didn't play. Whether it was bad grades in school or a bad relationship that was toxic for me, he wasn't having it. I can say with pride that I have taken a bit of every positive male influence and made it a part of who I am. Truly, that is the reason why I am such a strong woman. There are times when I dislike being a strong woman but it's all that I know to be especially after Mister's death. If I weren't strong through the grace of God, I would have crumbled like a cookie, and I would not exist today.

Intimacy

Celibacy is something I practiced for a very long time— seven years to be exact. I did it because if I was not attracted to a man, or if love was not involved, I didn't want it. I wanted to make love, not just have sex with a man. When I know I have that man who is deserving of my love and heart, I will definitely surrender to his love. I am not a selfish lover. It's not always about me. I love very unselfishly, and with this man, I could feel it happening.

We went on several dates, playing basketball, watching movies, and having dinner at restaurants. We spent so much quality time together. We were getting more and more familiar with each other and grew closer and closer. The time came around for intimacy.

In the beginning of our relationship, I had a problem with it. For some reason, I was afraid of getting close to him. I kept putting up a wall because I didn't want to show my real feelings. Love can make you very vulnerable. The thought kept coming to me. What if I fall in love again? I know for sure that if, God forbid, something happens to him, I won't be able to carry on this time around. I couldn't fathom the thought of losing him too. Negative visions always entered my thoughts.

Love is like a gamble, and I'm rolling the dice. The time came for us, and I finally decided to lay all the cards down. We were listening to the sounds of R. Kelly, and he grabbed me in his arms, and we started kissing. The feelings rushing through my body. Passion sparks exploding in the air, like it was fourth of July. Once we finished making love, we took a hot steamy shower together. It was so romantic, and intimate. My heart is falling in love again. Our relationship was growing, stronger and stronger.

Just like any other relationships, it wasn't always peaches and cream for us. We also had our trying moments. We were two people who were set in our own ways. Because of Mister, I was spoiled, and he was too. He was the oldest of his family, and I was the oldest of mine. I remember in my college psychology class, it was said that in a relationship, it is difficult for two people who are both the oldest child in the family to get along. I knew it to be true, but I wasn't going to let that dictate my relationship with him.

In the very beginning of our relationship, my heart wasn't responding to the feelings. I was numb inside. I was very much attracted to him, but my heart wasn't making that connection with my brain, and not because I didn't care about him but because that was how it is when your heart is damaged. For me, it was all about the fear of losing him, and because I was having problems opening up to him, the arguments came on.

How did he always know the exact buttons to

push? I was like a ticking time bomb ready to explode. I guessed because of what I had been through, I became this short-tempered woman. I knew that was not a good thing, but the reflection of my past made me this way. I just felt it was unnecessary for us to have arguments over silly simple shit, when I had bigger matters to worry about.

I had a business to build and money to achieve. I had my mind on my money all of the time. I was trying my best to advance from a damaged and broken heart. I was trying to put all the pieces of my heart back together, like a puzzle, but every time we argued, what it did for me is take me backward.

For every single step advancing, I went eight steps backward. Our arguments were basically over the struggle of power and control. Who had the upper hand? For instance, our exes became a major issue for the both of us. For me, I always made comparisons between my new love and Mister. I couldn't help it. He was so good to me. If Devon did something that I felt was inappropriate, something that I knew Mister wouldn't have done if he were alive, I would let him know it. I was always bragging and making comparisons to Mister until one day, he had just about enough of it. We had the biggest argument ever.

I was struggling with this relationship, with letting go of my past. I still kept a small photograph of Mister in a collage of pictures, along with myself, and my two dogs, Pepper and Stumpy. I didn't think he paid any attention to it, since it sat on my dresser, way out of the way in the corner. But of course, he did. He became very hostile about it.

"Damn it! Baby, would you please stop living in your past. I am here! I am your man. C'mon babe, you have to stop this, or we are not going to make it with our relationship!" he said.

At first, I really didn't see any harm in it. It was just a photograph of the past until he started to say, "What if I had my ex-wife's picture sitting on my dresser? You know for sure, you would be all up in my ass about it."

I listened to him, and I thought about everything he was saying. He was right. I would have been all up in his ass. The next morning, I began to really rationalize the situation. I knew I was wrong. It was pretty selfish of me, not to mention downright cruel. When I reflected back on it, I had to make myself realize: This was a new man with different actions and reactions. I have to love him for him. I needed to stop all of the comparing. I prayed for a man, and now that I have him, I was sabotaging our relationship without even knowing.

I prayed for a good man whom I could work with and build a future together, a man without any children. At our age, I especially knew that was going to be difficult. It was a special request from God. Now, he had granted my request again. When I thought about it all, this man was everything that I had prayed for. I decided it was imperative for me to make the changes that I needed to do in me, or I was going to lose him forever. I didn't want that.

The process of dating is not easy. I didn't want to start taking auditions and interviewing again for a new man. We had to make our relationship work. We just had to. With his red cape on and the word LOVE on it, he came into my life and rescued my heart and my soul.

Openly and expressly, I could say that I was ready to tear down the walls that were blocking and keeping us away from each other. I was ready to give my all to this relationship. I wanted to do all the things for him, like cooking breakfast, lunch, and dinner. I wanted to be there to encourage and motivate him. I wanted to love him unconditionally. I wanted to be his best friend, basically to take care of him, like a woman who is in love does for her man.

Then I realized everyone who has ever crossed my path in life hasn't been by mistake. This man came across my path for a reason. God brought us together for a purpose—love. God put all the right people in my life for a reason, and I knew then that he was the right man for me and that I was the right woman for him. I was put in his life to help him with some of his issues. I've fallen in love with him because he did make me want to laugh when I wanted to cry. Good laughter is something I hadn't done in years, and it felt so damn good to be laughing now. It was not so much about what he could give me materialistically.

I had that with Mister. I know how it feels for a man to want to give you everything in the world. With my new love, his love made me want to get up in the morning. Although I have my career, I was missing true happiness. Now I have it with him. I have the balance that I needed. In life, we never know what's going to happen to us or the cards that will be dealt—whether it's going to be a good life or a hard life. Only time will tell. Will our relationship survive, or will it all end? I don't know. But what I do know is that I am on the right track. I am ready to love again.

My Words of Inspiration

First off, let me begin by saying, "I am truly sorry for your loss."

From this moment on, your life is going to traverse a whole different direction. There will be plenty of moments of sorrow and despair until your wound heals. Time is an important factor; it is going to be a journey along a road to redemption and recovery. The grieving process is a period that you definitely can't rush. It takes time. I would never advise anyone to quickly start another relationship.

For some people that may work, but for me that is not the solution. My heart had to heal. How do you heal? For me, I keep myself involved. God, family, true friends, and work—they are my saviors. They give me the strength that I need for me to want to continue on in life.

Also, make sure you surround yourself with positive people. Before you know it, you'll be blessed again with love. It probably will not be the same kind of love that you had previously, but it will be the love that will keep you happy for long. So be ready!

The Advice

Ladies and gentlemen, there could be a flip side to my story for you whether you are the other woman or a man, in a relationship. Please take care of the situation. Handle your business properly—that is, to get Last Will and Testament in documentation. If there are any setbacks or problems, you will have the proof that you'll need.

There will be no objections. Plus, you will be protected and entitled to what your loved one wanted you to have. I didn't do so, on the account that I was young and in love, and my main focus was the fight against Mister's cancer. I tried so desperately to hold on to my superman, my love. I wasn't thinking about finances, and this is the price that I have to pay. Deep in my heart, I know that Mister took care of everything for me. I know he did. Sometimes in life, you get too comfortable with your wives, husbands, boyfriends, girlfriends, or any significant other.

You tend to take them for granted. You hear your spouse talking, but you're not really listening to what he or she is saying. Most of all, you don't show or express your love to them on a daily basis. But like they say, you never miss a good thing until it leaves you. I knew what I had with Mister. I had a best friend who made me laugh when I wanted to cry. He fixed any problems that I was going through in my life. He was my backbone. I never pushed him away from me.

One day, we did have a conversation about death. What would we do if it happened to us? The conversation actually came up around the time that I was in the hospital for my Myomectomy surgery. I lost a lot of blood that day but not enough for a blood transfusion. My mind went through a transformation. Before that incident, Mister witnessed a young woman who worked diligently, trying to get closer to her dreams. I was learning myself. Who was I? What was my purpose to this life? I knew of my talents and capabilities. I wasn't satisfied with the norm of working—that is, on a regular nine-to-five shift in work; it just wasn't for me anymore. But of course, at that moment of my surgery, he also witnessed the same strong woman become weak.

This was when he began to question himself about our relationship. What would happen to him if something happened to me? Will I be able to go on with my life? Would he be able to go on with his life? He assured me that his grown children would learn the truth of our relationship, because it would be the inevitable. Death is a topic that no one likes to discuss, but it is a part of life, and it is something that we all are going to have to go through and experience eventually. No one leaves out of here alive.

Death is a journey from this life to the next—a better life, an everlasting life. Life and the people in it are so precious, so never take your loved ones or anyone for granted. I never did.

www.ingramcontent.com/pod-product-compliance
Lightning Source LLC
Chambersburg PA
CBHW071851070526
44583CB00016B/1641